CHRISTIANS AND JEWS

A Psychoanalytic Study

By
RUDOLPH M. LOEWENSTEIN, M.D.

*Member of the Faculty
The New York Psychoanalytic Institute
Yale University, Department of Psychiatry*

INTERNATIONAL UNIVERSITIES PRESS, Inc.
New York   New York

Translated from the French
by Vera Damman

Copyright 1951
by
INTERNATIONAL UNIVERSITIES PRESS, INC.

Dedicated to the Christians who gave their lives for persecuted Jews

CONTENTS

Preface 9
Introduction 11

Chapter One

1. Anti-Semitism and Mental Illness 14
2. Anti-Semites in Psychoanalysis 26
3. Group Psychopathology 43

Chapter Two

1. Political Manipulation of Anti-Semitism 53
2. The Protocols of the Elders of Zion 59

Chapter Three

MOTIVES OF ANTI-SEMITISM   64

1. Xenophobia 65
2. Economic Factors 79
3. Religious Fanaticism 89
4. Anti-Christianism 102

Chapter Four

1. Jewish Character Traits 107
2. The Marginal Man 147
3. Psychoanalysis of the Jews 153

Chapter Five

ISRAEL AND CHRISTIANITY: A CULTURAL PAIR   181

Chapter Six

OUTLOOK FOR THE FUTURE   200

Bibliography 203
Index 215

Preface

The original manuscript was started in France in 1941 and was written in French. It was suggested then that it would be much easier to translate the text than to put something that was written in poor English into good English. This is the reason why I continued writing in French even after I had come to this country.

It took me several years to formulate the thoughts as they now appear in the present manuscript. During this time I discussed various aspects of the problem of anti-Semitism with colleagues and scientists in related fields. My understanding of the problem was greatly enhanced by these discussions and the valuable suggestions given to me. I wish to acknowledge my indebtedness particularly to Marie Bonaparte, Guy de Rothschild and Georges Halphen, with whom I discussed this problem in France. I owe many insights into the historical aspects of the matter to Horace M. Kallen and Robert P. Casey, and I have profited much, also, from the psychoanalytic discussions with Heinz Hartmann, Ernst Kris and Katherine Wolf.

For the manuscript itself I wish to express my gratitude to Aline Caro-Delvaille and particularly to Vera Damman, who not only translated the book but made many valuable editorial changes. I want to thank, also, Lottie M. Maury for her kind co-operation and help.

RUDOLPH M. LOEWENSTEIN, M.D.

New York, November 1950

Introduction

In August 1940, two months after the signing of the armistice between the Vichy Government and Hitler's Germany, I went to visit Madame Marie Bonaparte, the famous French psychoanalyst, in the south of France. We discussed the world political situation which was so terribly gloomy at that time. We also discussed the Jewish situation and the question of anti-Semitism. She told me of a recent conversation she had had with the director of an important periodical. She had reproached him for the anti-Semitic campaign he had launched at that time. He denied in reply that he had any personal anti-Semitic prejudices, pointing out that several of his intimate friends were Jews. She told me that he justified his paper's policy on the grounds that France was in a period of revolution and was going to need some one to blame; and the Jews, as usual, were the obvious scapegoats.

This conversation with Marie Bonaparte, and certain thoughts she expressed at that time, was the starting point for my research into the problem of anti-Semitism. Undoubtedly there were personal motives for making such a study. For what, naturally, would be the frame of mind of a man who, although born in pre-1914 Russian Poland, had for many years completely identified himself with France only suddenly to find himself morally rejected by his adopted country because he was a Jew. But I also had motives of more general validity. It occurred to me that experience in psychoanalysis, which deals with psychological problems in which emotional and irrational elements predominate, might contribute to an understanding of anti-Semitism. Anti-Semitism is such a strange, incomprehensible, many-faceted phenomenon, and can have such dire consequences not only for the Jews themselves but also for those individuals and nations who are contaminated by it, that it seemed important to find out if psychoanalysis could contribute toward an understanding of it and a solution of the problems arising out of it.

With this thought in mind I began to observe anti-Semitic reactions in my patients more closely, with some interesting results. I was able to trace most revealing connections between a patient's anti-Semitism and certain trends in his psychological development.

Since I knew from my own experience that anti-Semitism is also a phenomenon of collective psychology and that at certain moments in history it can spread through a country like a plague, I found it necessary to try to trace a connection between its manifestations in collective psychology and the psychoanalytic observations made on individuals. Furthermore, any facts brought to light by psychoanalysis had to be linked with the social and historical processes without which the individual psychological phenomena would never have occurred or would not have assumed such tremendous proportions. For anti-Semitism is no isolated or time-limited phenomenon—no mere offshoot of Hitlerism. It has existed for many centuries, either in a chronic state or intermittently, in most of the countries where Jews have settled.

I found it necessary, therefore, to review the whole history of anti-Semitism. Many books have been written on this subject, attributing anti-Semitism to one cause or another according to the personal point of view of the author: hatred of foreigners; the economic role of the Jews; religious fanaticism, and so on. In addition to such long-term factors I also had to consider the deliberate, cynically calculated use of anti-Semitism as a political weapon characteristic of totalitarian regimes today.

But even this was not all. In spite of the many distortions and surface contradictions that have characterized anti-Jewish manifestations through the ages, there has always been a certain underlying uniformity in what people have said about the Jews. I had therefore to examine the so-called Jewish "racial" traits. Throughout their history, how have the Jews reacted to their generally hostile environment? What have been the psychological interreactions between the Jews and the Christian world in which they have lived for so many centuries? Through a close examination of some of the peculiar features of these interreactions I think I have been able to trace the connections between the historical data and the psychological data uncovered through psychoanalysis.

This has led me to evolve the theory of a "cultural pair" formed by Jews and Christians, which is the basis for my explanation of the phenomenon of anti-Semitism.

In the following pages I have endeavored to set down the results of my research in the spirit in which it was conducted: one of complete objectivity, guided only by a regard for scientific truth.

Chapter I

I. ANTI-SEMITISM AND MENTAL ILLNESS

There is no exact definition of anti-Semitism, and no agreement on its symptoms. An attempt to diagnose it was made by a Russian doctor, Leon Pinsker, who in 1882 published a pamphlet entitled *Auto-Emancipation* in which he proposed the creation of an autonomous Jewish territory as a remedy for the desperate plight of his fellow Jews.

Pinsker's diagnosis of anti-Semitism can best be given in his own words:

> Among the living nations of the earth the Jews are as a nation long since dead. With the loss of their country the Jewish people lost their independence, and fell into a decay which is not compatible with existence as a whole vital organism. The state was crushed before the eyes of the nations. But after the Jewish people had ceased to exist as an actual state, as a political entity, they could nevertheless not submit to total annihilation—they lived spiritually as a nation. The world saw in these people the uncanny form of one of the dead walking among the living. The ghostlike apparition of a living corpse, of a people without unity or organization, without land or other bonds of unity, no longer alive, and yet walking among the living—this spectral form without precedence in history, unlike anything that preceded or followed it, could but strangely affect the imagination of the nations. And if the fear of ghosts is something inborn, and has a certain justification in the psychic life of mankind, why be surprised at the effect produced by this dead but still living nation?

A fear of the Jewish ghost has passed down the generations and the centuries. First a breeder of prejudice, later in conjunction with other forces we are about to discuss, it culminated in Judeophobia.

... Judeophobia is a variety of demonopathy with the distinction that it is not peculiar to particular races but is common to the whole of mankind, and that this ghost is not disembodied like other ghosts but partakes of flesh and blood, must endure pain inflicted by the fearful mob who imagines itself endangered.

Judeophobia is a psychic aberration. As a psychic aberration it is hereditary, and as a disease transmitted for two thousand years it is incurable.

It is this fear of ghosts, the mother of Judeophobia, that has evoked this abstract, I might say Platonic hatred, thanks to which the whole Jewish nation is wont to be held responsible for the real or supposed misdeeds of its individual members, and to be libelled in so many ways, to be buffeted about so shamefully.

If we disregard the obvious theoretical errors, such as belief in the direct hereditary transmission of psychoses and the confusion between phobias and psychoses, which were part of psychiatric thinking at the time he wrote his pamphlet, Pinsker's diagnosis agrees in certain respects with the findings of some modern psychiatrists. Within the last few years, for example, anti-Semitism has been classified by one psychiatrist, Dr. Richard Brickner, as one of the group of paranoid traits typical of the German people, and by Erik H. Erikson, it has been compared to syphiliphobia.

For readers who are unfamiliar with psychiatric theories and terminology it might be useful to give a brief description of what is meant by the terms "paranoia" and "phobia." A phobia is a neurosis characterized by irrational states of anxiety; these may be aroused by empty or closed spaces, by railway travel, by certain animals or insects; sometimes the phobia takes the form of an exaggerated and ungovernable terror of contamination—as in syphiliphobia. The victims of phobias are usually quite harmless human beings who, though unable to control their anguish or terror, are aware that these are irrational and a form of illness.

Paranoia is not a neurosis but a psychosis or form of insanity. A paranoiac may have the delusion that he is Napoleon or the Messiah; or he may have delusions of persecution and hold the firm conviction that he is the target of plots against his life or health. Sometimes, reversing the roles, he himself becomes the persecutor, attacking and killing the people he believes are plotting against him. Unlike the victims of a phobia, the paranoiac is convinced of the truth of his delusion.

There are evident analogies between the reactions of anti-Semites and the reactions of psychotics. There is a type of anti-Semitic behavior which is also to be found among neurotic or prepsychotic patients. The victim of the neurosis develops an attitude of suspicious vigilance and obsessive dislike and irritation toward some member of his household or entourage. Such symptoms occur frequently among people who are obliged to live together in too close proximity over a prolonged period—among prisoners of war, for example, or among members of a polar expedition confined in winter quarters.

Anti-Semitism stimulates three types of behavior which resemble the three clinical pictures described above:

1. An attitude of perpetual vigilance and distrust

of Jews, which may crystallize into overt and obsessive dislike.

2. Judaeophobia—a mixture of hatred, fear, contempt and disgust for Jews.

3. A "delusional" or "paranoid" form of anti-Semitism, the victims of which are convinced of the existence of a world-wide Jewish plot for the enslavement and destruction of the Aryan world.

Nevertheless, in spite of the many resemblances between anti-Semitism and certain forms of mental illness, there does not seem to be sufficient justification for putting them wholly on the same plane. There are neurotics or psychotics who are not anti-Semitic and there are anti-Semites who are neither neurotic nor psychotic. It can be affirmed, however, that anti-Semitism is very often one symptom of mental disturbance. Germans who attributed Germany's weakness to the nation's Jews and to the taint of Jewish blood in some of their citizens were reacting in the manner of phobiacs; the mental state of people who give full credence to the *Protocols of the Elders of Zion* bears a very close resemblance to a paranoid psychosis. But it seems to be a resemblance only. The Nazi leaders and the many other people who believed in the authenticity of the Protocols were not psychotics in the usual clinical sense of the word. They were not delusional on the same psychological level as mentally sick individuals whose similar forms of delusion necessitate internment. Likewise, Jüdaeophobia is not a phobia in the sense that agoraphobia and claustrophobia are forms of such mental illness.

On what grounds then can certain types of anti-

Semitism be described as "pathological"? Certainly there is a resemblance in the type of delusion. In both clinical paranoia and delusional anti-Semitism the delusion takes the form of a firm conviction that malevolent, invisible influences are at work in a conspiracy against the sufferer. And both in clinical phobias and in the narrower Judaeophobia, seemingly harmless objects or persons can provoke reactions of uncontrollable repulsion.

Efficiency is known to be impaired in people who are mentally sick. This is also true of the social mental diseases. People in the pathological group of anti-Semites are prevented by their obsession from seeking rational and permanent solutions to their social and economic problems.*

There are other resemblances: an individual with a phobia of wasps, even though he cannot overcome his terror, knows quite well that the chances are against his being stung and also that a sting is rarely dangerous. But the paranoiac, while retaining complete lucidity in all fields which do not touch his delusion, is inaccessible to reason and to factual evidence when his delusional ideas are involved. Inaccessibility to reason is also one of the most typical characteristics of the anti-Semite, who is unable to re-evaluate his opinions and prejudices in the light of factual evidence that refutes them. The passions and the unconscious motives and mechanisms involved in his anti-Semitic feelings are too powerful to yield to reason or experience.

* It is true that anti-Semitism can be manipulated to give temporary relief to economic and social ills. But it is reasonable to suppose that anti-Semitic solutions, like all other pathological solutions to men's problems, ultimately work to the detriment of the group applying them.

We find therefore that although anti-Semitism cannot be placed in any one of the well-known clinical categories it is nevertheless frequently an indication of some sort of mental disturbance that could be classified among the social mental diseases.

There are of course many types of anti-Semitism which have nothing in common with either phobia or paranoia. The French editor mentioned in the introduction to this book who launched an anti-Semitic campaign in his paper as a political maneuver, without himself believing a word of what he printed, was suffering from no delusion. And I wonder how many of the Nazi leaders really believed the accusations they made against the Jews. Their anti-Semitism was neither phobic nor paranoid, it was criminal. Jews were just victims of sadism and political ambition, who could be persecuted and pillaged and killed at will. Jews have frequently aroused sadistic hatred because they are persecuted and vulnerable. Man is strongly attracted by the possibility of assuaging his cruel instincts on defenseless victims; and when propaganda affords him not only the opportunity but also the justification for doing so, the temptation is overwhelming. This fact has been only too clearly demonstrated during the past decade, when killing Jews has permitted so many men to indulge their sadism with impunity and even with patriotism, while at the same time avenging themselves on the rich and powerful.

In the category of criminal anti-Semites there are many whose cruelty is clearly a kind of sexual perversion. Women anti-Semites are known to be both attracted and repelled physically by Jews. And for both sexes the tortures inflicted on them stimulate and satisfy, consciously or unconsciously, deeply rooted sadomasochistic desires.

Among the types of anti-Semitism that do not come into any of the above categories, there is the hostility towards Jews stemming from "racial" antipathy, such as the prejudice of a predominantly blond people against the dark-haired, olive-skinned oriental or "Latin" type, and vice versa. A like antipathy is common for people of different cultural or religious groups. Many Gentiles, particularly in non-Mediterranean countries, are repelled by the recognizably Jewish physical type or set of mannerisms, or by a "Yiddish" accent. It is important, when evaluating these reactions, to differentiate between those which are the result of a realistic appraisal of the psychological make-up of some individual Jews, and the purely emotional undiscriminating reactions of the Jew-conscious Gentile who thinks in stereotypes. Only the latter can truly be called anti-Semitic.

There are many people who have latent anti-Jewish prejudices which they try to dominate or restrain. Such individuals may make a distinction between two kinds of Jews: the "bad" Jew, with all his stereotyped vices of greed, avarice, cruelty, cunning, treachery, and so on, and the "good" Jew, who is pure and idealistic, noble and altruistic. Obviously this effort to divide the sheep from the goats is not an objective evaluation, for such people would never think of dividing Frenchmen or Americans into good and bad categories. They are apt to betray their underlying prejudices by such statements about Jews as "There's nothing of the Jew about him," or "He's no Jew." Thus consciously or unconsciously, even among well-meaning people, the very word Jew has come to be synonymous with all the vices which tradition and superstition have associated with the so-called "bad" Jews.

Furthermore, the unpleasant traits found in some Jews are attributed to the fact that they are Jews, and this in turn becomes an explanation of them. The belief that Jews are dishonest, for example, is not by any means always based on actual experience of the behavior of Jews in money matters but is often founded on impressions and preconceived notions weighted down with mythological concepts. When a Jew is dishonest, his dishonesty is dubbed "Jewish" and is attributed to Jews in general—a Jew is dishonest "because" he is a Jew.*

Moreover, quite apart from their "faults" Jews frequently arouse antagonism by traits which in non-Jews would be considered qualities: their initiative and enterprise, their intellectual or artistic endowments. Anti-Semitic reactions are often caused by jealousy and envy, and are always prevalent in that class of people for whom anyone possessing intellectual qualities is an object of superstitious dread and scorn.

There is a large group of people who are anti-Semitic through motives of expediency or self-interest. In countries where anti-Semitism is the officially prescribed attitude, political or social climbers will adopt it to further their careers or to improve their social standing. Civic courage is a rare virtue.

There are several attenuated forms of this tendency to howl with the wolves. Some people think that

---

* Charles Peguy, the well-known French writer, was thinking of this peculiar trait in the mentality of anti-Semites when he recommended them to try to imagine what they would say if a certain public figure whose honesty and patriotism were under suspicion were a Jew.

there must be some truth in what is said about the Jews since they provoke such intense antagonism. Others feel resentment toward the Jews because of their sense of guilt for the persecutions Jews have suffered at the hands of Gentiles, and try to find faults in the Jews to justify this persecution. Others resent them as eternal victims of injustices which they feel called upon to redress. Unwilling to assume this role permanently, they resent the Jews as a thorn in their flesh and cannot help feeling that their disappearance would make living with their own consciences easier. Finally there are the people who merely adopt the anti-Semitic tinge of their social milieu and justify their attitude by occasional sweeping criticisms of the Jews.

One of my patients recently wrote me the following most illuminating letter:

> My reactions to the recent Jewish successes in Palestine have come as somewhat of a surprise and relief to me. There had always been a conflict between a more or less socialist point of view, as well as a sympathy for the underdog, and an undercurrent of anti-Semitism, which as we know came from "way back." I took no position on the Palestinian question. Jewish nationalism is no solution I said. Of course under the circumstances, one couldn't help favoring the Jewish side, for all the various objective reasons, and then common justice demands that one ... but then it was always common justice demanding that one ... it was never any real sympathy for the Zionist cause.
> I just knew it was going to be just another one of those lost causes. They were going to get pushed around as usual and sold down the river. And I hadn't done anything about it. I wasn't going to do anything about it. But still it gave me a bad feeling. They were always on the spot, sort of hopeless, helpless, on my conscience, with their

hand outstretched and maybe looking in my direction. It was rather uncomfortable.

All these stories about Haganah and Irgun being well organized and representing a certain strength, were just stories. When the showdown came they'd be a pushover. It all seemed out of character and contrary to precedent. I thought of the Jews as eternal foreigners, city people who belonged behind a counter in some buying and selling game with a pretty high rate of profit in their favor. Not a very wholesome lot. Then always being herded into rather disreputable and dirty ghettos or worse, concentration camps—innocently of course. Always running with their tails between their legs from one tragedy to another. Everybody's stepchildren. I felt sorry for them and knew they were wronged. But I couldn't possibly identify with people like that, I couldn't really feel anything for their fool cause. Too many shopkeepers and too damn many martyrs!

Then there were all the other Jews—the super-Jews one heard so much about—all the big names. Most fields of science, the arts and politics seem slightly overloaded with "distinguished" Jewish names. I never resented their success. In fact I rather enjoyed the rather exotic touch and it more or less illustrated what I would have liked to believe that they were just as good as anyone else. If they seemed a bit better, I didn't really mind, it just made all that business about the ghettos and concentration camps harder to bear. The point is, that it didn't bring them any closer to home either. Einstein or Freud or any of those overtalented individuals don't remind me much of the people I know any more than those martyrs or the little greaser behind the counter. The fact of course that I do know a lot of Jews is beside the point. They were just friends, and my anti-Semitism, except in very veiled form was usually felt, or directed, against the Jews I didn't know. When I thought of "Jews" I just didn't think of regular ordinary people. They didn't have a history either, except of being kicked around, and they didn't have a country where you could "place" them like other people.

Then a few weeks ago, as the Palestinian situation began to reach a crisis, news of Jewish successes kept filling the papers. It was more than just resistance. These incidents began to look more and more like real military victories. Newspaper reporters discussed the relative military strength of both sides, with the general consensus of opinion putting the balance in favor of the Jews. This was a relief from the high-minded appeals of the liberal press. Maybe they were well organized after all . . . well equipped. I looked at the illustrations of the training camps with new eyes. They had suddenly become respectable . . . not a few desperadoes but people with an army like everyone else, fighting for national independence. From what the papers said it looked like a pretty good outfit. With half a break they could probably clean up on the Arabs. The bastards weren't a pain in the neck any more! They were just regular guys with a tough job on their hands.

I thought of the old Bible stories . . . the Promised Land, the Siege of Jericho, King David and all that. It was in a way part of my history too. I'd been brought up on that stuff. But somehow I had never been able to reconcile the hero tales of the Children of Israel with my other conception of the Jews. Now it all began to make sense. These were really the people the Bible was talking about. I didn't have to feel sorry for the Jews any longer. I could feel with them. I know how my grandmother would have felt. And I do too. "We stand at Armageddon, and we battle for the Lord."

So we see that there are all shades and varieties of anti-Jewish reactions and many types of anti-Semites, ranging from the group which merely thinks in emotional stereotypes or in terms of self-interest, through the more seriously contaminated group which has fixed delusions about the Jews, to the most dangerous group of all whose hostility towards Jews is translated into overt acts of criminal violence. The various types can be evaluated in terms of the degree to which they are able to submit their affective and emotional reactions to the control of reason and the evidence of reality.

This leads us to the fundamental problem. How and why do people become anti-Semitic? What function does anti-Semitism fill in the life of the anti-Semite? It is significant that both anti-Semitic and well-disposed Gentiles generally agree in attributing the same "unpleasant" traits to the Jews. But whereas the anti-Semites attribute them to all Jews and consider their anti-Semitism justified thereby, the well-disposed Gentiles confine their criticisms to the individual Jews who have misbehaved. It would seem, therefore, that the fact that a comparatively large number of Jews possessed certain unpleasant traits would not in itself be sufficient to provoke anti-Semitic reactions, though it often affords a pretext for the discharge of already existing, hostile feelings arising from other sources.

Some people are conditioned to anti-Semitism from earliest infancy in environments where it is chronic, and may grow up from childhood with an actual physical repulsion for the "Jewish" type. The antipathy of others may date from some disagreeable experience involving a Jew; it may be a souvenir of an unfair Jewish schoolteacher or of an unsuccessful rivalry with a Jew in an examination or a sports' event, or in a love affair or a business deal. Let us note, however, that when the offending person or the successful rival in such an incident is non-Jewish, the resentment remains localized on the actual offender, whereas if a Jew has been implicated the resentment spreads to all Jews.

It is quite evident, however, that personal and incidental associations cannot in themselves explain the appearance of anti-Semitism, nor can they contribute to an understanding of the underlying psychological forces at work in the mind of the anti-Semite. The psychoanalytic method, however, does give us a richer and deeper insight into the problem.

II. Anti-Semites in Psychoanalysis

Before we take up the problem from the angle of psychoanalytic observation on neurotic patients, let us remind the reader that psychoanalytic treatment of a neurosis consists in tracing the neurotic symptoms back to their unconscious psychological causes. The symptoms are the result of conflicts between various emotional tendencies and the forces which oppose them. They have their roots in early infancy, and among them by far the most important are those involving members of the family.

They are important because they are the first conflicts the child has to resolve in his first contact with society—through the family. It is through the family that he must learn to live in society with other human beings. The socializing process is accomplished by his gaining progressive control over the forces of his instincts—in other words, at the expense of the instincts. And the manner in which the child achieves this control will set the pattern for the type of solution he will apply in adult life to the emotional problems created by conflicts between his instinctual drives and the demands of the external world and of his own moral conscience. He will achieve this mastery through the use of psychological mechanisms which enable his ego to defend itself against the instinctual drives. Among these mechanisms the most important is repression. The purpose of repression is to hold in check unacceptable desires not only by preventing them from being translated into action but by banishing them from consciousness, and by repressing all thoughts, ideas or memories capable of arousing these desires. When the defense against these instincts breaks down, neurotic disturbances result. Disturbances also occur as a result of unsuitable or morbid solutions to the conflicts.

Needless to say, emotional conflict in childhood is not by any means the complete explanation for neurosis in adult life. The whole process of man's psychological growth and development is a series of conflicts and attempts to adapt to a changing environment. Conflicts which had been dealt with at an early age recur and have to be resolved again on a different level during the psychophysiological changes of puberty. And again in adult life the demands of society confront the individual with an entirely different order of problems. But when a man continues to apply his infantile patterns of solution to his adult problems, either through perseveration of these patterns or through reactivation of anachronistic reactions, neuroses result. Among the sources of neuroses the relative importance of factors deriving from childhood or puberty or adult life vary in every case.

Among the conflicts playing an important role in neuroses two are most directly connected with our subject: ambivalence, and the oedipus complex. We know that in the human mind love and hate are very closely, one might almost say inseparably, related, and that generally feelings of love are accompanied by feelings of hate for the same person. This phenomenon is known as ambivalence. During childhood the two components of this ambivalence become gradually and progressively separated. The child tends to repress and render unconscious any tinge of hostility toward the persons he loves and to withdraw all affection from the persons he dislikes. Little by little he creates personages who are wholly black or wholly white—angels or devils, heroes or traitors. Generally this process is not confined to childhood but continues into adolescence and sometimes into adult life. However, in the normal course of emotional development, the intensity of the ambivalence decreases considerably with age.

The ambivalence of the emotions is oriented in given directions from childhood. The child passes through one stage of development, essential in the formation of a normal adult, which Freud has called the oedipus complex: the stage when the little boy experiences erotic feelings towards his mother and feelings of jealousy and hatred toward his father. These feelings are subjected to early repression and seem to disappear forever. The normal adult generally has no memory of them.

The repression of these erotic and hostile drives toward the parents, and the consequent passing of the oedipus complex, form the nucleus of what will later become the moral conscience of the adult. The repression of the drives which form the oedipus complex is a process common to all human beings. There is no society in existence, however primitive, that does not forbid incest and parricide under threat of dire punishment. However, the very fact that this taboo is so absolute and universal indicates that the forbidden desires exist and that the possibility of these acts remains. They have been reduced to unconsciousness and apparent impotence, but they nevertheless continue to exert an indirect influence on the human mind.

The impulses inherent in the oedipus complex are repressed in the child both through fear of punishment and by affection for the rival parent. But the work of repression goes much deeper than this. The child sets up forces within himself which fight the oedipal desires by means of an internalization of the parental taboos; he constructs parent images which represent for him the morality of human society. He then no longer needs pressure from without to resist the forbidden desires. He has formed what Freud called a "superego," the nucleus of his moral conscience.* In neuroses the defenses fail partially and the drives tend to overwhelm the ego.

Psychoanalytic treatment aims at inducing the patient to recall the deeds and events, desires and unconscious conflicts—now forgotten or banished from consciousness—which have caused his neurotic disturbance. By giving the patient freedom to express all his thoughts and feelings without any constraint, the psychoanalytic method gives access to the unconscious regions of the personality. The imprints left in childhood on the psychological development of a human being manifest themselves when reactions which originated in the past are found to perseverate in later life

* The id, the ego and the superego, as defined by Freud, are the three parts which compose the psychic apparatus. They are conceived of as systems of psychic functions. Functions of the id center around the basic needs of man and their striving for gratification. Functions of the ego mediate between these strivings, the outside reality and the moral demands around which center the functions of the superego.

and when there is a tendency to repeat these reactions.

Now in the course of this reliving of the past there is a re-enactment of the reactions of that period, but this time with the psychoanalyst as the object. Freud called this the "transference" to the psychoanalyst of feelings or emotional reactions which had originally been experienced toward people in the patient's entourage. During these transference reactions, erotic and aggressive tendencies are brought to light and also the ego forces which combat them. The ego defenses, in fact, play a very significant part in the course of the analysis. They form the basis of the unconscious resistance which the patient sets up against his treatment and his cure.

What light can psychoanalytic observation of patients throw on the origins and causes of anti-Semitism? The cases which are best known to us and which furnish particularly good opportunities for studying the problem, are those in which the patient exhibits only a latent or moderate degree of anti-Semitism when he comes for treatment. The interesting thing about such cases is that during the course of the analysis these mildly anti-Semitic patients will suddenly reveal strong anti-Semitic prejudice. Psychoanalytic treatment, therefore, offers a good opportunity for a kind of experimental study on the incipient and developmental stages of anti-Semitism.

At some point in the course of analytic treatment almost all non-Jewish patients will manifest varying degrees of anti-Semitism. Almost invariably their reactions confirm Pinsker's observations that the Jew is regarded with a combination of fear and hate, and as a dangerous, mysterious, disturbing and uncanny personage. These fear and hate reactions become directed toward the analyst in the process of transference. In other words, the patient transfers to the analyst the fear and hate feelings which date back to his childhood and which were originally directed toward his parents. And when the analyst is a Jew these feelings are attributed to his Jewishness and take the form of transitory anti-Jewish reactions. During these anti-Semitic stages of analysis, the Jew who is hated and feared by the patient in the person of his analyst usually represents to him a deformed image of his father or even of himself.

It should be emphasized that this fearsome figure of the father corresponds only to one part of the patient's feelings toward his real father and usually to an unconscious part. In fact, it is the very patient who is conscious only of admiration and respect for his father who has repressed all his aggression toward him since childhood. We have already explained the importance of ambivalence. It tends to split the father image into two personalities, the "good" father and the "bad" father. In religion the split is into God and the Devil and in art into Hero and Villain.

During analysis, when the transference is "negative"—i.e., dominated by hostile feelings once experienced toward the father—the Jewish doctor is regarded as the dangerous and sinister Jew. In this sense he can be said to represent to the patient the hated and feared father. Frequently, however, another person who represents authority and who can readily be identified with the analyst is substituted for the father.

I observed a striking example of this mechanism in a young Frenchman whom I analyzed in France in

1940–1941. He was in his twenties, was violently anti-German and apparently devoid of all anti-Semitic prejudice; in fact, anti-Semitism seemed to him typically *boche* and hence particularly detestable. In the course of his analysis he had a dream of a man in a German uniform but with Jewish features, with whom he had to fight to the death. He admitted shamefacedly that in his imagination he had confused me with the enemy who had become both *boche* and Jew. He then recalled that during his scouting days he had been unfairly treated by a Jewish superior. At the time he had generalized his resentment into an attitude of distrust of all Jews. Later he had overcome this attitude but it revived momentarily during analysis when the question of rivalry with his younger brother aroused in him bitter feelings towards his father whom he reproached for preferring the younger son. Under cover of this transitory anti-Jewish reaction he could express with impunity a resentment felt in childhood.

The mechanism of "displacement" which operates in transference is a common enough process in everyday life. Pent-up anger against a superior can safely be vented on an innocent inferior: an unhappy woman may "take it out" on her children, a resentful maid on her employer's dishes. In psychoanalysis the analyst takes the rap for all the patient's accumulated aggressions of childhood, adolescence and even maturity.

Another defense mechanism against the instinctual drives is "projection." Projection, like displacement, plays a big role in normal life also, but it is to be seen with particular clearness in paranoia and related psychoses. Paranoiacs may believe, for example, that others have incited them to sexual acts which they have committed or have desired to commit. Firmly convinced of their own innocence, they blame others as their tempters or as the instigators of their thoughts and actions. The medieval monk who saw in every beautiful woman an incarnation of Satan was projecting his own suppressed desires.

During analysis projection becomes a complex clinical mechanism. We have seen how repressed desires must be brought into the open in order to surmount them. Patients struggle against becoming conscious of these desires by attributing them to the analyst. At such moments the Jewish analyst may be regarded as a "dirty Jew," sensual and diabolical. Other patients have similar feelings toward the analyst when the analysis begins to free them from the infantile fixations which have occasioned their difficulties. In such stages the patient revives anti-Semitic prejudices long since discarded and apparently overcome. In all these cases the mechanism is the same. When the analysis threatens their pathogenic compromises, they begin to hate and fear the psychoanalyst.

When the patient feels threatened by his own inadmissible instinctual drives he may protest that it is the analyst's fault because with his dirty Jewish imagination he has put such thoughts into his head. This is in miniature a paranoid form of delusion very common among anti-Semites.

Sometimes the neurosis has been built up on passive tendencies repressed in childhood. Neurotics of the passive type often overcompensate for their tendencies by identifying themselves with heroes or by imitating strong, virile characters. In such cases, when the neurosis breaks through in spite of all efforts at compensation, the analyst has to uncover the repressed passive tendencies to enable his patient to surmount them. Then there occurs a special type of fear reaction—fear that the analyst wants to weaken or emasculate them, or to change them into women. Curiously, in the minds of such patients during this phase the Jewish analyst is conceived alternately as a mephistophelian personage or as an effeminate, emasculated man. The fact that the Jews are circumcised and so in a sense mutilated stirs up in them superstitious horror, thereby revealing their unconscious fear of being mutilated or castrated as a punishment for forbidden desires.

In some patients the analyst can observe at first hand the sadistic satisfaction derived consciously or unconsciously from the idea of Jews being tortured and massacred. The structure of this type of satisfaction is very complex. Neurotics who suffer from an intense sense of guilt and who live in anticipation of punishment protect themselves by projecting their faults onto the Jewish analyst or onto Jews in general. They would like to see the Jews tortured and punished in order not to feel guilty themselves. To avoid punishment they would like to assume the punitive role themselves.* All such patients think and act at certain moments like fanatical anti-Semites. They make the Jews the scapegoat for their own repressed desires, both sadistic and masochistic.

The reactions of habitual anti-Semites have the same psychological structure as these transitory manifestations of anti-Semitism that occur during analysis.

Naturally not all neurotics react in these ways, nor

* Cf. Robert C. Bak: Masochism in Paranoia, *Psa. Quart.*, XV, 1946.

do all react with the same intensity during the course of analysis. What sorts of people, then, tend to have these strong reactions? One type is represented by the man who always tends to protect his self-esteem against any undesirable trait in himself by attributing that trait to others. All around him, in his family and among his acquaintances, he detects his own faults and inadmissible intentions. Men of questionable honesty, for example, are quick to accuse others of dishonesty or double dealing. These are the neurotics whose reactions are tinged with paranoid traits.

Another type which becomes an easy prey to anti-Semitism is represented by the man who tends to make a clear-cut separation between his aggressive feelings and his positive, affectionate and amorous feelings. Such people are more prone than others to think in terms of the completely admirable or the utterly detestable, and to show marked ambivalence in all emotional relationships. They think in sweeping generalizations and stereotypes. Some of them alternate between love and hate toward the same person, according to whether their vanity is wounded or is flattered at the moment.

Probably the great majority of fanatical anti-Semites belongs to one of these two types, which are often combined. But in their ranks are also found individuals who have been profoundly disillusioned by personal or professional disappointments and failures which they blame on others. They are quick to pick on successful Jews as their scapegoat.

It is impossible to determine the relative importance of the respective factors of inner propensity, specific development or cultural influence in the conditioning of these reactions. Probably all three factors are involved concurrently.*

The factors which produce anti-Semitic reactions in analysis are, of course, also operative in the case of Jewish patients and of Gentile patients analyzed by Gentile doctors. In the Jewish patient the same defense mechanisms come into play; he has the same tendency to generalize, but the threatening attributes of the analyst are not associated in his mind with his being a Jew. I have been told by Gentile analysts, however, that their patients sometimes experience anti-Semitic reactions towards them because psychoanalysis is considered a "Jewish" psychology, because its founder, Freud, was a Jew. In general, however, Jewish patients of Jewish analysts or Jewish patients analyzed by Gentiles make generalizations of a different order; they accuse their analysts of moral obliquities which they attribute to "all doctors" or "all psychoanalysts."

These differences arise from the fact that it is customary and traditional to react to Jews in the way we have just described as typical in certain stages of analysis. In western society the traditional concept of the Jew as scapegoat is always available. In patients who are devoid of any conscious anti-Semitism it is sometimes necessary to overcome considerable resistance in releasing anti-Jewish sentiments into consciousness. It is important, incidentally, not to confuse latent anti-

* A remarkable study of the correlation between anti-Semitism and other personality traits has been made by Elsa Frenkel-Brunswick and R. Newitt Sanford (*The Anti-Semitic Personality: A Research Report*). Another extensive study is being prepared under the direction of Nathan Ackerman and Marie Jahoda, drawn from material collected by various psychoanalysts. We hope that these and other studies will bring about a better understanding of the interplay of the various factors involved.

Semitism with such normal transitory reactions as any man has from time to time towards an out-group.

Among the many patients who have assimilated this traditional concept of the Jew as scapegoat from their family and environment, there is one class which is particularly interesting. It was Freud's explanation of anti-Semitism in his book, *Moses and Monotheism*, which gave me an understanding of these patients. Christians regard Jews as the murderers of Christ. According to Freud, by loving and deifying Jesus the Christians feel relieved of the guilt feelings common to all mankind, which arise from death wishes against one's father. Jews who refuse to recognize Christ as God appear to Christians as unrepentant parricides.*
Among Catholic and Protestant patients I have noticed that there are various theories, on a conscious level, about the role of the Jews in the life and death of Christ. Some Christians have always been aware of the intimate relationship between Jesus and the Jews of his times. Some are conscious of a bond between the Jews of those distant times and those of the present day. Others recall that when they learned Bible history they thought of the Jews solely as murderers of Christ. And among the latter some have such a strong sense of the link between the past and present that they consider Jews of the present generation and of all future

---

* Freud used the psychoanalytic method of reconstructing from observed data the forgotten past of an individual's life to approach the "forgotten" prehistoric past of humanity. In his book, *Moses and Monotheism*, he applied this method to the very subject with which we are dealing. This book, which contains many penetrating ideas about the nature of Christian anti-Jewish feeling, expands his earlier hypothesis of the father's murder by the primal horde. He applied this hypothesis to the relationship of the Jewish people to their leader, Moses, who, according to Freud, was killed by his followers. Guilt for this deed created in their descendants peculiar submission to God.

generations guilty of the death of Christ. There are of course very few people in Western Europe or America today who still hold these convictions. But they were commonly held in the Middle Ages, and even in our epoch they furnished the reason for the pogroms in Czarist Russia and in Poland.

The patients I have in mind in this connection are those whose reactions toward the analyst are extremely complex, and center around the relationship between Christ and the Jews. The contradictory reactions exhibited by these patients in the course of analysis are derived from conflicts of the so-called "latency period" —conflicts to which religious instruction gives particular shape.*

To understand what happens in such instances we must go back to the psychological development of the child. The stage which follows the formation of the superego has been called by Freud the latency period. This is the stage in a child's life when the sexual drives are more or less in a state of quiescence. It lasts until the emergence of these drives in full force at puberty. During the latency of the sexual drives, and probably because of it, the child is able to proceed along the path of emotional and moral socialization, a process required of him at this age by his family and by society. The six-year old starts going to school and begins his moral and religious education. He may be considered to have reached the "age of reason" when his

---

*During a discussion of the relationship between faith and the psychoanalysis of religious concepts, a believing Christian maintained that the two were perfectly compatible: "Man becomes aware of God through his human faculties, therefore his religious concepts are given human expression, and this human expression may properly become an object of scientific psychoanalytic study."

superego is formed, but even then his moral development is not complete, and his superego must continue to be built up and strengthened by moral training through the years that follow.

At first the moral requirements of the superego are narrow and rigid. Its gradual adaptation to the social and psychological situation of later life necessitates complicated elaborations on conscious and on unconscious levels. Thus the moral requirements and prestige of the parents will come to be partially replaced by those of teachers, or of social, political and religious authorities. Admiration for the parents and a tendency to identify with them, especially with the father, yield to admiration and identification with heroes and, most important of all, to worship and faith in God.

Religious teaching is actually one of the most powerful means employed by society to effect the necessary elaboration and consolidation of the superego in the child. Through it, the moral principles representing the demands of the superego can be projected outward, thus becoming infinite and universal. The imperfect, real father is replaced by the perfect, universal God the Father.

Conflicts typical of the end of the latency period center around the need of the superego to hold in check the instinctual drives which tend to become turbulent before the onset of puberty. Among Christian children, initiation into religious life in their first communion intensifies this conflict between the instinctual drives and the moral forces, by accentuating repression. A temporary asceticism and feelings of intense guilt may develop in them, with accompanying rebellious drives which may take the form of religious doubts or sacrilegious obsessions.

The religious instruction given to a Christian child, whether it results in neurotic symptoms or not, leaves a deep impression on the patterns of his developing superego. It includes a study of Bible history, since the gospel stories supply prototypes for his moral formation. He is taught to renounce his aggressive instincts and his sexual temptations under threat of punishment in hell, and he is also taught to renounce them for love of Christ. He learns to love Christ and to identify with him. He is told that if he succeeds in repressing his bad instincts Christ will love him.

The Jews, who are described in the gospels as unbelievers and executioners of Christ, become in the imagination of the child so taught the symbols of these bad instincts, the incarnation of every wickedness the child has repressed in himself. On the other hand, since the Christian child identifies with the Son of God, God the Father whom the Jews recognize becomes associated in his mind with the Jews. The Jews are pictured in his mind as the "elders," the older generation—in other words, they become the transformed image of his own father. Thus the ancient conflict between Christ and the Jews which took place nineteen hundred years ago reflects the child's own past conflicts with his father, and becomes the unconscious symbol of his oedipus complex.

It would perhaps be more correct to say that these religious problems have their psychological counterpart, since it is on a psychological level that the conflicts of the preceding oedipal period are revived in the latency period by religious teaching. The fact that the

Jews represent to the Christian child both his own repressed instincts and his father, whom he fears and loves and hates at the same time, is the basis of one of the primary forms of ambivalence toward Jews; i.e., a mixture of hatred, fear and attachment.

While believing the Jews guilty of Christ's death, Christians cannot help being aware of the close ties which unite the Jews to Christ. The Jews are of the same race as Christ; they saw him; they participated in his death and they witnessed his resurrection; so that in the Christian imagination Christ and the Jews have come to be associated more or less consciously.

Christians must also reckon with the fact that Jesus became the Redeemer only because he was crucified. However violently they may denounce the Jews, the fact remains that the Jews performed the act which alone made Christianity possible. Their role has therefore been odious but indispensable throughout the history of Christianity, since they have borne on their shoulders the curse for the death of Christ. On a spiritual level the young Christian benefits by the crucifixion. On a psychological, unconscious, level the crucifixion represents to him the culmination of the unconscious death wishes of his oedipal period. The Jew is held responsible for the crime from which the Christian reaps moral and psychological benefit in redemption from sin. Thus the Christian child learns not only that the Jews were essential to Christianity in the past; he learns that they can serve even now as the scapegoat for the personal sins of every Christian.

This special role of the Jews in the history of Christianity as well as in the development of individual Christians, based on the father-son relationship, is also the source of that other type of ambivalence toward the Jews which consists of gratitude and deep resentment. It is also the source of the intensely ambivalent feelings experienced during analysis toward the analyst, if he is a Jew, by patients who have passed through such infantile conflicts.

Let me make it quite clear that by no means have all the Christian patients I have analyzed experienced all the conflicts described above. In many cases, certainly, such conflicts remain vague and inarticulate. Furthermore, in a great many cases the patient has formed his concept of the Jew from opinions derived from cultural and economic sources outside the sphere of religion. There is, however, one important fact to be noted. Among most patients who are only moderately anti-Semitic or whose anti-Semitism is only a passing phase during analysis, the symptom disappears more or less entirely once the analysis is finished, along with the other symptoms of the neurosis that have been resolved. In my opinion, the disappearance of the symptoms is not so much due to gratitude toward the analyst as to the fact that their oedipus complex was formed before they had received any religious instruction, which is given in the periods of latency and prepuberty. Their concept of the Jew, therefore, was only a superstructure over primitive conflicts deriving from the oedipus complex. The Jews, therefore, do not necessarily represent the epitome of all evil to all Christians. They can, however, do so under the pressure of pathological factors, individual or social.

In fact, the importance we have attributed to those cases in which anti-Semitism derives from the role attributed to Israel in the gospels, does not depend on any special intensity of anti-Jewish prejudice. There may exist perfervid Christians whose religious training has induced intense anti-Semitism, but I have not analyzed any. My experience with the Christians I have analyzed has been that, whereas their religion provided them with a pretext for hating the Jews, it also offered them the means to overcome this hatred.

It is true that nowadays religious education is rarely the sole or the main cause of fanatical anti-Semitism in an adult. It is equally true that the historical bases of anti-Semitism are far from being the main cause of the recent violent epidemics of anti-Semitism. The particular interest and significance of the cases I have just described, however, lies in the fact that in these specific cases the concept of the Jew as an object to be hated was not acquired fortuitously—as the result of some chance experience in life—but derived historically from the concept of Israel in Christian religious teaching which is the core of the traditional concept of the Jew. The concept of Israel in the Christian religion has this importance for three reasons: first, because it is implanted in childhood; secondly, because it is so widely accepted in a civilization which has been deeply influenced by Christianity; and lastly, because historically speaking it is one of the most ancient of the traditions that have been handed down through generation after generation, from antiquity to the present day.

III. Group Psychopathology

At certain periods in history there have been sudden flare-ups of anti-Semitism. The world has just passed through such a period—in fact, has not quite emerged from it. People who had seemed immune, but who must have had some latent prejudice, all at once became intensely anti-Semitic. During the past two decades we have had occasion to observe how this change of attitude sweeps over a country like a tidal wave, and how it overflows into neighboring countries as soon as social or political events favor its spread. It is quite impossible to attribute this simultaneous change of attitude on the part of so many people to purely personal causes in each individual case. It can only be explained either in terms of "mental contagion," or by the simultaneous appearance in a great many people of common psychological factors predisposing to anti-Semitism. The latter would seem to be the more valid explanation.

The symptoms of acute collective anti-Semitism are not very different from the symptoms in isolated cases. Frequently a collective outbreak is preceded by a state of "Jew consciousness"—a state of mind that easily develops in a state of suspicious watchfulness, which is one of the precursors of active anti-Semitism.

The superstitious beliefs of anti-Semites are a measure of their fear and hatred of the Jews. In the Middle Ages, the Jews were regarded as sorcerers, murderers, cannibals, enemies of humanity. In all seriousness they were credited with the most extravagant abnormalities. It was commonly believed that they had tails, that male Jews menstruated, and so forth. A few of these beliefs have persisted down to our times; there are still people who believe in the diabolical attributes of Jews. In the olden days Jews were accused of ritual murder and of unleashing the Black Plague by means of their sorceries; in our time they have been accused of sucking the blood of the "Aryans," and of sending them off to kill each other in wars.

The Christian theological concept of the "Jew" as it gradually crystallized during the early centuries of Christianity, was derived from an identification of the Jewish people with two personifications of evil: Cain, who murdered his brother, and Judas, who betrayed Christ for money. The identification of the Jews with Judas probably had a great deal to do with their being forced into the role of usurers in the Middle Ages. To these traditional preconceived ideas modern anti-Semitism has added the idea of sexual perversion. In Nazi Germany a special paper was founded for the purpose of warning the "chaste and innocent" Germans against these sexual perverts who derived diabolical pleasure from raping Aryan women.

Other traditional superstitions about the Jews were less violent. They were identified with Ahasuerus, the Wandering Jew. According to the well-known legend, Ahasuerus was condemned to wander eternally over the earth without a place to rest his head, for having refused to let Christ rest on the way to Calvary. In popular belief the whole Jewish people was under this curse; they could not rest and they could not die. Thus the superstition gradually took root that the Jews were the Living Dead, ghosts out of the remote past. The Church helped to confirm this belief by assigning them the role of "living witnesses of the true Christian faith," regarding them as eternal contemporaries of the life and the death of Christ.

In Christian belief the Jew is under a curse. In man's unconscious anyone under a curse is "taboo," in the primitive sense of the word: it is dangerous to approach too closely because of the evil which emanates from him. From this it is a short step to credit the tabooed one with all sorts of evil potentialities to justify his being shunned and driven out.

It is interesting to note that the legend of the Wandering Jew first made its appearance in the thirteenth century, at the very time when mass expulsions of Jews from Western Europe were in progress. The myth provided the Christians with historical and religious justification for expelling them.*

Man's tendency to generalize, and to simplify and personify forces of nature or whole nations is certainly at the root of the Jewish myth. The aggregate of individuals of Jewish origin is treated as a single individual: the mythical, diabolical Jew. Superstition has composed him entirely of vices, without a single redeeming human quality. For if all Jews were personified in one single Jew it is natural to credit this single Jew with all the vices and crimes of individual Jews composing the whole, even as we hold an individual responsible in his total personality for all his acts. This tendency to personify natural forces or groups of people corresponds to the "mythical" stage in the development of the human mind. It also corresponds to the need men feel to project on the outside world the im-

* Similar currents of collective psychology made their appearance in France after the defeat of 1940. Many Frenchmen began to talk of the Jews as a "nomadic" people. Obviously this was an attempt to justify in advance the anti-Semitic decrees to be promulgated by the Vichy government. It was also a convenient way for the French people to rid themselves of any sense of guilt, for surely it is in the nature of nomads to "move on." The anti-Semitic decrees, therefore, could be regarded simply as the natural consequences of the migratory tendencies of the Jews.

pulses and emotions which they vaguely sense within themselves.

Another aspect of the Jewish myth is the delusion of Jewish solidarity. Anti-Semites are so convinced of this solidarity that they come to think of the Jews as an indissoluble whole, directed and governed by mysterious leaders, the legendary Elders of Zion. A corollary is the belief that there exists a united Jewish financial clique, fantastically rich and powerful, which backs Jews in all walks of life; any differences in religious opinion, economic interests or national allegiance are conceived as nothing but a blind to deceive the gullible Gentiles; underneath their apparent differences all Jews are one and of a kind. Another widely held belief is that the Jews are invariably untrustworthy; that they always have proved and always will prove treacherous to any nation or individual who trusts them.

Let us examine in more detail the underlying mechanisms which generate and augment the aggressive forces of the masses, since intensification of mass aggression is at the root of all collective outbreaks of anti-Semitism.

The very young child has no moral scruples whatsoever against striking people or grabbing their possessions; in fact, he derives a great deal of satisfaction from both activities. Learning to curb these aggressive drives is a painful and difficult educational process, but most children are eventually so successful in repressing them that the average normal adult is quite unaware that he has these antisocial drives within him. Only those elements of his aggressive drives which are compatible with and desirable in the life of a society normally remain consciously in force—the competitive spirit in business or love, for example, or the fighting spirit demanded of its citizens by a nation at war.

We know that there are people who as individuals would be incapable of acts of violence but who nevertheless can be stimulated to a pitch of tremendous aggression when they are members of a crowd. This mass transmission of emotion has sometimes been attributed to a sort of mental contagion and sometimes to the power of suggestion. Freud, in a study of what he called "organized masses," stressed the fundamental importance of the relationship between the members of a group and their leader. On the basis of common love for their leader, members of such an organized mass build up a mutual identification, and there is a consequent reduction of in-group aggressions.

On the other hand, the very nature of the psychological bonds which bind the members of the group to their leader greatly increases the potential of violence against outsiders or out-groups. The leader, in fact, takes over the superego functions of his followers. The problem of dealing with their instinctual drives and disposing of their aggressions is now delegated to him. And when he decides to direct them against a victim of his choosing, their violence knows no moral bounds, since it is he, their leader, who fills the superego functions. Freud took the army and the church as examples to illustrate the psychological structure of organized masses. But a far more striking example would have been Nazi Germany.

Modern societies are to a great extent built up on similar structures, although here an ideal or an abstract principle often takes the place of a flesh and blood leader, and the mutual identity within the organized mass is based on a common belief or on common ideals. Other, less stable groups are formed on different bases, such as community of economic interest. In all cases the resultant identifications favor the development of hostile reactions towards outsiders who do not "belong."

Inversely, a common object of hatred seems to be especially propitious for incubating a "mob spirit," which in turn feeds and fans the flames of hatred of each member for the common enemy.

The psychological mechanisms described above are at the basis of collective outbreaks of anti-Semitism. Common hatred for the Jews, who are singled out as aliens and as "enemies within the gates," creates a state of mind comparable to the mob spirit. It accounts for the extreme violence of the group aggressions and for the fanatical tenacity with which anti-Semites cling to their delusions about the Jews in the face of disproof. Members of the mass are driven by powerful psychological motives to join the ranks of the Jew-haters and Jew-baiters. Apart from the satisfaction to be derived from a sense of superiority, they have a profound need to hate in common so that they may hate with a clear conscience. And lastly, belonging to such a group fulfills an important psychological function for many of them: it substitutes for their own psychological disorders a social mental disease which is much easier to bear.

Anti-Semitism considered as a social phenomenon cannot be interpreted in terms of the sum total of individual reactions. When social conditions are stable individual acts of anti-Semitic violence may have no general repercussions. On the other hand, quite mild manifestations among a certain group of individuals may have wide social repercussions. For example, the snobbish type of anti-Semitism prevalent in North America has led to the exclusion of Jews from many social and professional activities.

The case of Hitler is an example of the opposite process. Here the anti-Semitism of a single pathological individual had incalculable repercussions because of his enormous power. It might be argued that he obtained this power in the first place because his anti-Semitism struck a responsive chord in the German people. There is undoubtedly a reciprocal interdependence between the personality of a leader and the group which chooses him as their leader—between his influence on the group and the response of the group to his influence. However this may be, the fact remains that it was Hitler's anti-Semitic laws and his subsequent orders for arrests and persecutions that caused many Germans to translate their latent aggressions into overt acts of violent anti-Semitism.

All major outbreaks of anti-Semitism have been characterized by an intensification of group aggressions against a group regarded as different, and all have been accompanied by the superstitious beliefs described above.

The aggressive forces of a group are known to be intensified in times of poverty, unhappiness, discord and danger. There are many reasons why the Jews have so often been the targets and the victims of increased aggressions, which became organized into systematic and widespread anti-Semitism. In the Middle Ages one reason was the attempt of the Catholic Church to unite Europe under its aegis, which naturally led to an increase of hostility against the Church's enemies, among them the Jews. Another was the fact that the Western European nations in the throes of formation found anti-Semitism a useful political weapon. Furthermore, the special nature of the economic development of Europe at that time favored its increase. In modern times, exacerbated nationalism and the many political, social, economic, psychological and religious upheavals have all contributed to create what Freud called the "discontent of civilization" and Peguy the "malady of the modern world." Collective anti-Semitism occurs whenever the pressure of social, economic or political problems becomes unbearable, and can be temporarily relieved by discharging the accumulated tensions on the Jews.

There is an analogy here with neurotic illness. The difference between a normal person and a neurotic is that the latter is incapable of finding satisfactory solutions to his life problems; his reactions are not in terms of the reality situation. Similarly, during a wave of anti-Semitism, essential social problems are ignored, and individual conflicts with individual Jews are displaced onto that mythological entity, "the Jews." Hatred of the Jews, who are blamed for the difficulties, obscures the real issues. Anti-Semitism, therefore, owes its peculiar violence to the displacement of the aggressive forces generated in the masses by real social problems. Usually this displacement is produced artificially, by political manipulation, for the purpose of distracting public attention from the real issues.

In the case of individuals, frustrations are known to be conducive to neurosis. Similarly, social conditions which bring frustration and a sense of insecurity to a large number of people may produce analogous psychological group phenomena. The threat, or actual experience, of social upheaval, war or unemployment, destroys the psychological equilibrium of the group.

Generally there is a preliminary period of distrust in which, according to Ernst Kris, there are two separate elements: the first, distrust based on a critical perception of the contradictions between the professed ideals of the group and the real conditions of life; and the second, distrust due to the externalization of unconscious inadmissible desires within the individual himself. A state of generalized distrust may be considered a premonitory symptom of the psychological disturbances described in this chapter as typical of the disease of anti-Semitism.

Chapter II

I. Political Manipulation of Anti-Semitism

Among the many manifestations of the crisis through which western civilization is passing, one of the most illuminating has been Nazism. Nazism demonstrated how propensities towards collective violence inherent in all times of internal crisis could be systematically used for the furtherance of demagogic aims. And Nazism has been chiefly responsible for the extraordinary spread of anti-Semitism in our times.

The technique of using collective violence as a political weapon was by no means a Nazi invention. It had been used many times before throughout history. Nazism, however, is such a typical example of this technique, and also such a well-documented one—still fresh in our memories—that we do not need to go further back.

Among the many problems that faced Germany after the war of 1918, one of the most important was how best to deal with the humiliation of defeat. The German people had had an unbounded admiration for their army and its leaders and their defeat was a severe blow to their national pride. Some Germans reacted with a complete change of sentiment, and despised their erstwhile idols. Others met defeat by denying it. They claimed that the German army had never been beaten: that defeat was the fault of the socialists and the Jews. These particular Germans, by contriving thus to keep military honor unblemished, were able to regroup their loyalties around the old idea of an invincible army.

Long before the First World War there had been anti-Semitism in Germany. And after the war, the fact that the Jews were better able to adjust to the new democratic regime stirred up deep resentment among Germans of the old school, still smarting under their defeat. The next step was to accept the myth that the Jews had wanted the defeat, and after that to believe that they had engineered it. Thereby the Germans saved their national pride and the revered German army was exonerated.

In his article entitled "Hitler's Imagery and German Youth," Erik Erikson pointed out that before the war there were two extreme trends in German culture, one towards what he called a "too wide" cosmopolitan type and the other towards a "too narrow" German type. These types still existed after 1918, but their numerical strength had been reversed. The "narrow" Germans had been proved wrong, and so the "too wide" Germans came into temporary ascendancy. With astounding rapidity many Germans now became cosmopolitans, western democrats, or Russophile communists. It is certain that the German Jews were among those who turned more readily, and perhaps more sincerely, to these democratic or communist movements. Nevertheless a considerable number of German Jews remained "narrow" German, and would have become ardent Nazis if Hitler had not been anti-Semitic. This can be deduced from the number of Italian Jews who became Fascists and of French Jews who became Petainists. For once they have been assimilated into a country, Jews feel the impact of the various political and social movements within their country on the whole just as strongly as do their Gentile compatriots.

As we know, some time after 1918 a reverse movement set in and National Socialism once more replenished the ranks of the "narrow Germans." Cosmopolitanism was then denounced as the embodiment of the Jewish mentality.

The Nazis worked ardently and assiduously to clear Germany of her war guilt. Hitler realized that he could not make Germany into an aggressive nation again until he had rid its people of their sense of guilt and converted their "masochism" into "sadism" against foreigners, restoring to them once more the ideal of the invincible German army. During this process of reversal it was essential to restore the lost prestige and rehabilitate the values of "narrow" Germany. To quote Erik Erikson:

> . . . under the leadership of Hitler, Germany decided to cling to a few German absolutes, with monomaniac pride, determined ignorance, and blind brutality. She felt that she had to free herself from all the relativity of values from a "too wide" cultural experience.

Erikson sees German anti-Semitism as a projection of German weaknesses. They could no longer admit to an "inferiority complex" nor recognize the relativity of values implicit in cosmopolitanism, both of which are common Jewish tendencies—the former because of the traditional Jewish status of outcasts and the latter because Jews have been obliged so many times throughout their history to adapt to a succession of "host" countries that they have developed a sense of the relativity of national absolutes.

Hitler hated and feared criticism. His aim was to

imbue the German people with the absolute values of Germany's superiority, invincibility, and mission as the "Master Race," and for this he needed a completely submissive mass, dedicated to obedience. The critical insight typical of so many Jews became, therefore, the chief target of attack. It was regarded as the supreme Jewish vice and the scourge of the Jew-ridden democracies.

There is always a tendency for a nation in a state of ferment and change to syphon off internal dissensions by directing them against a selected target. This device obviously played a role of the first importance in the anti-Jewish campaigns in Germany after 1918. It was imperative to eliminate all discord and strife so that the German people could identify wholeheartedly with the image of conquering heroes. They were told by Hitler that they had not been defeated on the field of battle, but by the dissident foreign element in their midst: by the Jews and by the Jew-tainted Germans.

The Jews thus became the target of all the accumulated bitterness of the German people. As the "inner enemy," depicted at one and the same time as a capitalist sucking the blood of the Aryan race and as a revolutionary communist, they became the focal point for the aggressions of all groups. By persecuting the Jews the money classes and the lower middle classes hoped to exorcise the bogey of the dreaded revolution —and incidentally to rid themselves of their competitors and pocket their money. At the same time the working classes believed that they were at last throwing off the yoke of their exploiters.

The bond of German unity might have been established in common hatred of the victorious foreign allies, but Hitler was too shrewd a politician to attack the allies openly. It was just as efficacious and less dangerous to create an enemy within the nation on whom the Germans could wreak all the vengeful hatred they were not yet strong enough to wreak openly on their still formidable victors.

It follows that the "inner enemy" of a whole nation becomes the inner enemy of the individuals composing it. Thus the Jews came to personify Evil, and all the ignominious defeats man suffers in his struggle against his instincts could be blamed on them.

And here we touch on one of the fundamental aspects of the play of forces implicit in aggressive reactions. An unhappy nation, its latent aggressions exacerbated through suffering and insecurity, needed an outlet for its resentment. The Jewish minority, weak, but imputed to possess mysterious power, provided the Nazis with the necessary scapegoat and the perfect means for dissipating disruptive elements within the nation. The Jews were made responsible for defeat and for the postwar chaos. All the failures and inadequacies of the German people were transferred to the Jews. The Germans themselves had done no wrong, had shown no weakness. By this one maneuver the Germans were freed of disgrace, guilt and remorse.

There are striking analogies* between the ensuing persecution of the Jew and the expulsion of "evil" among primitive peoples. To quote Frazer:

> The notion that we can transfer our guilt and sufferings to some other being who will bear them for us is familiar to the savage mind. It arises from a very obvious confusion

* See Marie Bonaparte: *Les Mythes de Guerre*. London: Imago Publ., 1946.

between the physical and the mental, between the material and the immaterial. Because it is possible to shift a load of wood, stones, or what not, from our own back to the back of another, the savage fancies that it is equally possible to shift the burden of his pains and sorrows to another, who will suffer them in his stead. Upon this idea he acts, and the result is an endless number of very unaimiable devices for palming off on someone else the troubles which a man shrinks from bearing himself.

We will deal with the origin of the Jewish role of scapegoat in a later chapter. But the fact remains that, whether or not the Nazi leaders were sincere in their anti-Semitism, the anti-Jewish sentiment of the German people furnished Hitlerian Germany with its most powerful political weapon in the building of the new order.

Propaganda played a tremendously important role in Hitler's campaign. The influence of anti-Semitic propaganda can be compared to the influence of tradition, with the difference that propaganda is able to magnify its effect on the masses out of all proportion. It succeeds best in groups or countries where the aggressive forces of the masses are intensified by unsettled conditions. But only when these forces are manipulated by powerful groups for political or economic ends can they erupt into violent collective outbreaks of anti-Semitism.*

---

* It now seems that Nazi propaganda was not nearly so effective as was believed at the time. According to Kris, Speier and Leites, the German government reported as spontaneous popular demonstrations against the Jews what were in reality organized raids carried out on prescribed dates by disciplined groups. Hitler had more than propaganda at his disposal; he also had power. Anti-Semitism was obligatory. Few Germans had the courage to defy the totalitarian regime, so that perhaps many Germans acted with more violence than they really felt.

II. The Protocols of the Elders of Zion

The leaders of National Socialism in Germany made political use in both the national and the international field of the latent and overt anti-Jewish sentiment which was already prevalent in Germany and in other countries. The way had been prepared for them by a pamphlet which had been widely disseminated between the two World Wars: *The Protocols of the Elders of Zion*.

As is well known, this book purports to reveal the existence of a secret plot for world conquest organized by the mysterious and imaginary leaders of Judaism. The revelations can be summed up as follows: The aim of the Elders of Zion is to discredit religion; to spread subversive ideas among the youth of the world; to stir up and keep alive class hatred; to encourage luxury and vice in order to ruin the upper classes, already weakened by overtaxation; to incite the fury of the masses against the moral turpitude and degeneracy of the governing classes; to develop industry at the expense of agriculture and eventually to create huge industrial monopolies which will swallow up private fortunes and destroy financial stability; to stimulate and maintain economic crises so that at the appointed time they can unleash the final cataclysm after which the universal Judaeo-Masonic dictatorship will emerge, bringing to the world a *pax judaica*.

The Protocols were not a German invention. They had first appeared in the form of a printed broadsheet in Russia, and, according to Rollin, at the instigation of the Russian secret police, which was thoroughly versed in the use of such forgeries. Other editions appeared in Russia between 1903 and 1914. By 1935 it was estimated that several hundred thousand copies were in circulation in Europe and America.

In 1921 the correspondent of the *London Times* in Constantinople, Mr. Graves, pointed out that the Protocols were an almost literal translation of a pamphlet which had originally been written not as an attack against the Jews at all, but against Napoleon III. It had been published in Brussels in 1864, under the title *Dialogue in Hell between Montesquieu and Machiavelli; or the Politics of Machiavelli in the Nineteenth Century*. The author was one Maurice Joly, a brilliant but long since forgotten publicist and pamphleteer.

The legend of a Judaeo-Masonic world plot played a very important role in international politics between the two World Wars. The victims of the myth were by no means only to be found in the gullible masses: they included some well-known and highly influential personalities, among them Count Lansdorf, General Ludendorff, Alfred Rosenberg, Adolf Hitler, William II, Houston Chamberlain, Admiral Kotlchak, Henry Ford.*

Perhaps one day we shall have sufficient knowledge to diagnose the causes of economic and social disturbances as well as we can now diagnose the causes of epidemics. When that day comes the myth of the Judaeo-Masonic plot will seem just as absurd to us as does the medieval myth that held the Rabbis responsible for the Black Plague.

---

* When Henry Ford learned that the Protocols were a forgery he retracted his opinions and withdrew the publication he had made of them in the United States.

The success of the Protocols is to some extent comprehensible when considered in the light of the alarming social and political events of the period. Three empires—the Russian, the German and the Austrian—had been overthrown; Lenin's revolution was at its bloodiest; the Third International had just been formed with its threat of world revolution; there were communist uprisings in Bavaria and Hungary. Men everywhere were confused and alarmed by catastrophic events that were beyond their comprehension. Their superstitious dread of the unknown was aroused, and they seized on the Protocols, which explained these disturbing phenomena as the machinations of occult and malevolent forces working toward the destruction of mankind.

There is documented proof that the Protocols had the impact of a revelation on many of the Nazi leaders—a revelation, in fact, that strangely resembles the hallucinations experienced by some paranoiacs which start a chain reaction of a whole delusional system. Adolf Hitler was smitten with the "Protocol psychosis," and developed its principle themes in *Mein Kampf*.

Regardless of whether all the Nazi leaders sincerely believed in the authenticity of the Protocols, they certainly provided the Nazis with invaluable ammunition. They helped stimulate anti-capitalist hatred not only in the working classes, but also in the white-collar classes which had been impoverished by the war. They helped to exacerbate nationalistic sentiment, festering since the defeat. And the fact that Jews were scattered throughout the nations of the world gave the Nazis a chance to interpret the hostility of the democratic governments toward National Socialism as the result of Jewish influence and Jewish domination in those countries. The Protocols also facilitated their foreign propaganda, whose purpose was to "honeycomb" a country by dividing public opinion and winning support for German policies.

The psychological device employed by the Nazis was very simple. By the constant juxtaposition of the terms communism, socialism, Freemasonry, capitalism, and international Jewry, these diverse concepts came to be regarded as one and the same thing by the man in the street. By this device of identifying the different and the contradictory they not only reached the enemies of communism and socialism but also the Catholic enemies of Freemasonry. Socialists and communists were reached through this identification of the Jews with international capitalism, as were innumerable people of no strong political or religious convictions but with latent anti-Jewish prejudices. Thus the Nazi propaganda insinuated itself into the minds of many different groups of people and managed to fuse the enemies of each into a common target.

One cannot help being struck by the number of analogies between the alleged methods of the "Elders of Zion" and the actual political methods of National Socialism. Moellendorf has called the Nazi accusations against "international Jewry" a projection of Hitler's own intentions. Israel was supposed to aspire after world domination, with the rest of the peoples reduced to slavery; National Socialism openly proclaimed that Germany was the Master Race with the right to dominate the other, inferior, races. And the sinister alliance between capitalism and revolution attributed to the Jews was a valuable double-edged weapon in the battery of Nazi propaganda, with its promise to both the capitalists and the proletariat that their enemies would be destroyed. And under cover of their accusations that the Jews engineered wars, their secret preparations for a huge war machine progressed unsuspected.

This projection device served as a perfect blind. The procedure is strikingly like the behavior of a "persecuted-persecutor" type of psychotic. Many Germans convinced themselves that they were acting in legitimate self-defense, thereby attenuating the sense of guilt attached to their own aggressions.

Nevertheless the idea of a secret nucleus of Jewish leaders has been accepted with extraordinary naïveté and gullibility by many people who do not consider themselves anti-Semitic. Whenever there is economic or political tension in a country, whenever situations change and fortunes are lost for no tangible reason, there may occur a regression to the fantasies of youth, and to explanations based on "mysterious plots." And where there is potential or latent anti-Semitism, what is more natural than that the mysterious plot should crystallize round the myth of "world Jewry."

Hitler through his propaganda was able to foment similar delusional notions in the common man in almost every country. He numbed the critical faculties of the public in the countries destined to be his next victims. He appeased the last scruples of his own people against plunging Germany into war. In the eyes of his fifth-column admirers within the intended victim country, Hitler's victory would deliver them from a mysterious and dreaded danger: Hitler attacking the Jews became in the eyes of his admirers St. George attacking the Dragon.

Chapter III

MOTIVES OF ANTI-SEMITISM

The recent scourge of anti-Semitism could never have spread so fast nor become such a sinister and powerful political weapon if anti-Jewish prejudice had not already existed in a chronic state in many countries in Europe and America.

The life conditions of the Jewish people have always been quite different from the life conditions of any other people. Jews have been discriminated against by the surrounding peoples, socially, politically or economically; and at certain moments in history this discrimination has taken the form of active persecution and sometimes of massacres.

Psychoanalysis has shown that most human actions are motivated not only by the consciously recognized causes but equally by another whole set of motives of which the individual is not completely aware. These motives are particularly powerful in all intensely emotional reactions. Anti-Jewish reactions are pre-eminently of this type.

Among the various groupings that different writers have made of motives of anti-Semitism, I propose for purposes of simplification to use the following:

1. *Political Anti-Semitism:* as described in the previous chapter.

2. *Xenophobic Anti-Semitism:* based on the common human phenomenon of group hostility to outsiders.

3. *Economic Anti-Semitism:* the complex of anti-Jewish reactions engendered by economic factors.

4. *Religious Anti-Semitism:* based on the intolerance of members of one religious group toward those of a different faith.

A psychological phenomenon, however, is rarely the product of a single set of factors but is generally the result of the interaction of several. This "overdetermination"* is particularly marked in a phenomenon like anti-Semitism. All the separate elements enumerated above are simultaneously involved in the various types, though the proportions vary according to the period, country and people involved. It would perhaps be more exact to say that any one type of anti-Semitism could always be placed in any of the other categories, but for purposes of convenience in describing them it is simpler to classify them as above.

I. Xenophobia

Xenophobia, or hatred and fear of foreigners, is a very frequent, if not a general, phenomenon. Under given conditions, racial, national, religious or cultural minorities tend to become targets for the dislike, distrust and antagonism of the majority. The threshold of tolerance toward minorities varies according to the character of the majority and to social, economic and political conditions.

Generally speaking, the higher the value set on certain collective ideals, the stronger the hostility toward any deviations from them. In a group where re-

---

* Freud used this term to bring out that psychological phenomena are usually determined not by one but by several concurrent causes.

ligious faith has a strong affective value, religious minorities are liable to provoke intensely hostile reactions. In a group where racial pride ranks high, racial differences such as skin color may stimulate contempt and antipathy. In a group whose national independence is in jeopardy, total subordination to the national interests is exacted and any other interests or loyalties are considered treasonable. Needless to say, the threshold of tolerance is determined by a great many other factors as well. There is also considerable variation in the criteria whereby the majority accepts into, or excludes from, its group, individuals from a minority group.

Much anti-Semitism comes within the frame of reference of xenophobia. As already stated, the probability of anti-Semitic reactions increases in times of general unrest and insecurity, or whenever conditions intensify the pent-up aggressions within a group.

Hatred of a minority group such as the Jews is sometimes counterbalanced by factors belonging to another collective ideal, an ideal perhaps which permits of identification with Jews. For example, a common hatred of another "foreign" group may create a bond with the Jewish group based on national or simply on human solidarity.*

The attitude of a majority group toward a minority depends to a certain extent on the characteristics of the latter, not only on its numerical, economic or political strength, but also on its general attitude toward the majority. There are two quite distinct types of minorities: the minorities who are despised

---

* The positive attitude of most Frenchmen towards Jews under the Nazi occupation is a good example of such an identification.

and looked down on because they are considered worthless or inferior, and those who are admired and imitated because they are considered superior to the majority. Among the latter are the governing, aristocratic or wealthy classes, or—in countries like the United States—the descendants of the earliest settlers. As a general rule the Jews have not belonged to this type of admired minority.

A group which is considered to be an "inferior" minority, but which is anxious to assimilate with the majority, may be looked down on but is rarely hated. On the other hand, a minority which clings to its own differences and distinctive traits and yet expects all the barriers against assimilation with the majority to be removed, may encounter considerable antagonism. Antagonism may also be aroused by the attitude of the minority toward the majority. The fact that the Jews often maintain an attitude of fear and distrust toward the Gentiles has certainly at times increased hostility toward them.

It is important to stress the point that the Jewish minorities differ in many important respects from other religious, cultural or national minorities. A religious minority is generally formed by a group which either clings to an old form of religion abandoned by their coreligionists or breaks with the traditionalists to adopt a new form of faith. The Jews are neither of these minorities. Nor are they in any country a national minority with sentimental loyalties in another state; nor are they an elite minority descended from conquerors or colonizers. The Jews have settled in many countries, but wherever they are they constitute a unique type of minority.

According to Toynbee they are "fossil remnants" of the Syriac Society who have survived in the western world. Together with the Monophysite Christians, the Nestorians and the Parsees, the Jews belong to what he calls the "penalized minorities." But they even differ from these other penalized minorities in having no country or parcel of ground to call their own and in having lived in a state of permanent exile for two thousand years.

Because of their homelessness the Jews have been considered by the surrounding peoples—and have frequently considered themselves—a special, and lately an inferior, "race." The notion of race has played a part of first importance in the persecutions to which they have been subjected.

To anthropologists the term "race" means large human groups having in common certain combinations of physical features traceable to their common heredity: the shape and proportions of their skulls, faces, noses; their skin and hair color, etc. However, the term "race" has given rise to so much misunderstanding and has been so misused that some anthropologists would like to banish it from the vocabulary of their science. Neuville, in his "Peuples ou Races" points out that the term has a conventional value only, since the many migrations and crossbreedings of the human species have determined purely artificial groupings, and no clearly defined races. All that can be said is that among people grouped into various nations there has gradually evolved a homogeneity based on community of traditions and habits.

The white race, to which the Jews belong, is generally considered by anthropologists to be the issue of the crossbreeding of several races during thousands of centuries. One of the most usual classifications, though not a universally accepted one, distinguishes three main racial strains in Europe—the Nordic, the Alpine and the Mediterranean, from which have issued all the various European peoples. Anthropologists believe that the so-called "Aryan race" is the result of a linguistic or cultural unity imposed on the ancient peoples of Europe by Asiatic invaders speaking an Indo-European language. The Germans, Hooton has remarked, probably have no greater proportion of Nordic blood in their veins than have the Israelites.

Anthropological studies have shown that there are just as many variations in shape of skull and nose, and in color of hair and eyes, etc., among Jews as among Gentiles. When Jews have been domiciled in a country for several generations certain Jewish physical types become almost indistinguishable from the native type. This approximation in type may be due either to the participation of Jewish groups in the original formation of the "race" in question, or to later crossbreeding with the native population, or to the influence of such environmental conditions as climate or diet. The general opinion seems to be, however, that the convergence of Jewish and non-Jewish types is more likely to be due to a blending of the two populations than to the influence of the physical environment.

The famous hook nose is far less common among Jews than is generally supposed. It was apparently a foreign accretion in the first place, acquired by a crossbreeding of Palestinian Jews with Hittites and Armenians. According to Hooton, the characteristic Jewish features are the result of a blending of three racial strains: the Mediterranean, the Alpine and what he calls the "Iranian Plateau" strain.

History contains many examples of the common ancestry of Jews and non-Jews. The Israelites interbred with the Canaanites and the Philistines, the latter of Aegean origin. Palestine was conquered by many diverse peoples who left their imprint on the physical characteristics of the population. Large segments of the populations of the Mediterranean Basin, the Black Sea and the Caucasus were converted to Judaism, after the Babylonian exile, or several centuries later when Palestine was reconquered by the Jews under the Asmonean dynasty, or later still when Judaism was well on the way to becoming the universal religion. During the latter period large numbers of Syrians, Egyptians, Greeks and Romans were converted to the Jewish faith. Let us not forget that during the first century A.D. the Jewish world population amounted to nearly seven million people, of whom only a million and a half lived in Palestine. At that time every tenth Roman was a Jew. It was only in the year 135 A.D., after the Romans had crushed the revolt led by Bar Kocheba, that severe restrictions were imposed on proselytism by Jews and on mixed marriages between Jews and non-Jews.

When we consider that a great many of the first Christians were Jews and that many Jews in Palestine and neighboring countries became Christians and as a result fused with the surrounding populations, when we take into account also the tremendous number of Jews forcibly or voluntarily converted to Christianity during the course of long centuries of persecution, it is not hard to understand why there are so many physical likenesses between Jews and non-Jews. In fact, it may well be that some of the most fanatical anti-Semites in Germany, France, Italy and the Anglo-Saxon countries have more Palestinian Jewish ancestors than do the Jews they persecute.

The Jewish physical type is, however, often quite distinct from that of their neighbors. The features considered characteristic of Jews are a thick or hooked nose, slightly prominent eyes, thick lips, wavy or crinkly hair. These features are equally characteristic of the various Mediterranean types. But among the Jews there is a further undefinable "something different," so that even when they have none of these typically Jewish features, they are still frequently recognizable.

The modern "Jewish" physical type has been evolved through centuries of crossbreeding and through segregation and exclusive in-group marriage during the past few centuries. There are, therefore, certain "family resemblances" among Jews of particular regions: it is often possible to distinguish German Jews from French Jews, Polish Jews from Russian Jews, and so on.

During the past few years some anthropologists have had great hopes of establishing the fact of racial differences through a study of the blood groups of different peoples. The Nazis, obsessed as they were with the idea of "Aryan blood" and "Jewish blood," sought on the basis of such studies to prove that there is a specific Jewish race. There was nothing, however, in the results of this research to establish any difference between Jews and other peoples of the white race. In fact, the Jews were found to have blood characteristics almost identical with those of their host populations.

In Hungary, for example, the Jewish blood group index was almost equal to that of the other Hungarians, whereas that of the Transylvanian Germans who had been in Hungary for several centuries differed quite appreciably from the blood group index of the Hungarians and still had the characteristics of their ancestral German group.*

The Nazis went to such lengths to try to prove their theory of a Jewish race because they felt the need to justify their exclusion and persecution of the Jew on scientific grounds. There was also another factor, which can be deduced from the number of interdictions governing sexual relations between Jews and Germans. The sexual factor is one of the most powerful unacknowledged motivations underlying anti-Semitism. In anti-Semitic literature the Jew was represented as a sexual pervert who took pleasure in raping and debauching "Aryan" women.

We have seen from the description of the anti-Semitic reactions of patients in the course of analytic treatment how this image of the Jew as a sexual pervert represents a projection of the ill-contained desires of the person himself. These representations are often associated with Jewish circumcision, which may be a source of unconscious attraction for non-Jewish women but also of strange mystery and repulsion for both sexes. It accounts for the violent sexual jealousy manifested by most anti-Semites.

Social psychology can clarify for us some aspects of this complex phenomenon. We know that in every type of society, whether primitive or cultured, there

* Cf. J. D. Bruzkus: The Anthropology of the Jewish People. *The Jewish People*, Vol. I, New York: Jewish Encyclopedic Handbooks, 1946.

are laws limiting the choice of the marriage partner. In existing civilized societies, sexual relations between parents and children or sisters and brothers are forbidden. Such taboos do not entirely eliminate incestuous desires, however, and a great many of man's neuroses stem from psychological conflicts arising out of the taboos. In most of our societies there is also another type of restriction concerning marriage and sexual relations: a tendency to frown on marriages between persons of different religions, nationalities or social strata. Foreigners in particular are often severely ostracized, especially if they belong to a different "race." Now it is this very ostracism which makes them particularly desirable sexually. We know how often in nations of mixed religious and ethnic groups there is a tendency to choose an illicit lover in the different group and a marriage partner within the group. The attraction a man feels for a foreign woman is often irresistible because it corresponds to his desire for the forbidden love object. Paradoxically, in his psychological development, this forbidden love object replaces the person in the family closest to the child—the mother or sister for the boy, the father or brother for the girl. And it is because of this transfer of feeling from the incestuous love object to the foreigner that the latter can so easily become an object of intense jealousy, guilty fascination and repulsion. Here is a good illustration. Under Hitler sexual relations between Germans and Jews were qualified as incestuous and therefore strictly forbidden. Yet at the same time Hitler went to extremes to prove that the Jews were of a totally different race from the Germans. This contradiction is particularly revealing in view of the role played in Hitler's life by his unconscious attachment to his mother and sister.*

All these are contributory factors in determining why some individuals are singled out as aliens and become the target of the ambivalent reactions of the majority. They all play a significant part in modern anti-Semitism and also in anti-Negro reactions in North America.

But quite apart from these psychosexual aspects, there has always been a close connection between anti-Semitism and xenophobia. However, the anti-Semitism of antiquity had very little in common with the special mixture of morbid fear and loathing which the Christian world has manifested toward the Jews.**

From the time when the Roman Empire adopted Christianity as the state religion the Jews became an ostracized minority, and ever-increasing restrictions were imposed on their social and economic activities. Their situation rapidly deteriorated after the fall of the Roman Empire, and during the Dark Ages they lost the citizenship rights granted them by the Romans and became the personal chattels of sovereigns and princes, since in the fledgling nations of Europe only Christians were granted citizenship. It was then that the Jews became "aliens" in the modern sense of the word. Their gradual isolation into a separate ethnic

---

* Cf. G. Kurth: The Jew and Adolf Hitler. *Psa. Quart.*, XVI, 1947.

** Gradually economic and cultural competition between Greeks and Jews within the Roman Empire became more pronounced. Still, it remained a normal type of competition. However, the fact that Judaism was the only monotheistic religion in a polytheistic world gave rise both to attraction as well as suspicious hostility. The hostile attitude persisted—although the motives in the meantime changed—but they provided in later centuries the content of accusations by those Christians who were directly influenced by the Greco-Roman civilization.

group was partly the result of legal and economic sanctions which placed them outside society, but partly also because they considered themselves a distinct ethnic community.

Nevertheless, for many centuries the Jews lived in amity with their neighbors in almost all parts of Europe, thanks largely to the wisdom of their religious leaders; for when the Roman measures became more repressive the Jewish leaders authorized Jews living in dispersion to conform to all the laws and customs of the countries where they had settled, so long as they observed the three fundamental laws of Judaism: they must have no other God but Jehovah; they must not practice incest; they must not commit murder.

Up to the time of the French and American revolutions which placed the concept of nations above religious and ethnic unity, the Jews were the only non-Christian group tolerated on Christian soil, though it is true they had to live as outcasts, in ghettos, and were periodically subjected to persecution, pillage and expulsion.

Toward the end of the eighteenth century their situation was gradually improving, first in Austria, then in France and finally, after Napoleon, in most of Europe. In fact, they seemed well on the way to complete legal and moral emancipation everywhere, except in reactionary countries like Russia and Roumania.

Contemporary anti-Semitism is essentially racial in its manifestations. Even Jews who had long since broken all social and religious ties have been thrown back into the group of persecuted undesirables. And even in countries like the United States, where there are no discriminatory laws, social barriers have been set up which keep the Jew at arm's length and tend to relegate him to a separate ethnical group.*

From the point of view of emancipation and basic equality, the modern epoch has brought severe setbacks. The tremendous flare-up of anti-Semitism under the Nazis, with the slaughter of over five million Jews, has strengthened the conviction among Jews and non-Jews alike that their assimilation into western civilization is well-nigh impossible.

Many people consider the Jews themselves responsible for their treatment as aliens. They point, among other things, to the food laws of the Jewish religion forbidding them to eat with non-Jews. This is interpreted as withdrawal and nonco-operation, if not as actual hostility. For in man's unconscious, the act of "breaking bread" in common has profound affective significance. Sharing a meal implies the abandonment of egoistic, aggressive feelings toward the guest, since the primitive instinct is to keep everything for oneself. Anyone who refuses to eat at the same table rekindles in the depths of unconsciousness the instinctive attitude of suspicion and hostility that has been repressed, not without difficulty, in favor of a hospitable and generous attitude. Such a refusal is interpreted symbolically as a desire to withdraw from the community.

We have seen that in some countries Jews are hardly distinguishable from the surrounding population. In countries such as France and Italy where they are in the process of total assimilation, and where, moreover, there was considerable resemblance to the

---

* Baron remarked that if at this date all Jews were to convert to Christianity they still would not be accepted as fully privileged Christians, but would probably come to form a new group of "Jewish Christians."

native population in the first place, the "Jewish type" tends to disappear. In Eastern Europe, however, the situation is quite different. There the Jews have lived in compact closed communities, concentrated in specific areas, and consequently most of them were easily distinguishable from the surrounding population both in language, dress, customs and religious rites.

It is true that the Jewish religion does contain what might be called "national" elements. The Hebrew language is used in religious offices. There are religious festivals to commemorate events in Jewish history, so that Judaism is not a religion pure and simple but is also associated with the Jewish nation.* There are many Jews, however, who would deny this statement. Devout Jews will say that for them Judaism is a religion and nothing else; others that their only ties with Judaism are ties of traditional morality; others again would only admit to a certain attachment to family traditions. All would affirm their loyalty to the country of which they are citizens. Yet this does not prevent ultranationalists in their various countries from ignoring all but the traits which mark the Jews as "aliens."

There is no doubt that ultranationalism—that unfortunate outgrowth of the concept of national sovereignty—has been an important source of modern anti-Semitism. It operates through the medium of xenophobia, which is its counterpart. It has added fuel to the already highly inflammable potential of mass aggression described earlier. Members of an ultranationalistic group are just as closely knit together as members of a crowd. Their leader may be a man or a

* *The Jewish Encyclopedia*, VII:359. Judaism.

set of national ideals, but the result in both cases is intense hostility toward foreign countries and toward "foreigners." And as, in the child, aggressive tendencies are kept in a state of repression by the forces of sympathy, affection or admiration, so, in the adult, love and admiration for those who belong to the same nation facilitates the repression of in-group aggressions. But at times when things are not going well in their country the same factors cause them to react with intense hostility toward foreigners or toward any person or group who appraises their difficulties with critical objectivity. They prefer not to be made aware of the real causes of tension and discord. It is the very function of ultranationalism to divert and disguise internal disruptive forces.

The almost inevitable result of exclusion is to render Jews "Jew-conscious"; i.e., self-conscious—perpetually on the defensive and unsure of themselves. It dilutes the identifications they had built up with their Gentile compatriots and strengthens those with their companions in misfortune. Their special characteristics are thereby accentuated. They become all the more conspicuously "different." Like other excluded minorities, they become nationalistic in their turn, and even ultranationalistic. All this of course serves to heighten the xenophobic anti-Semitism of the majority. Once more there is a vicious circle, almost impossible to break.

Nevertheless, modern anti-Semitism cannot be explained solely in terms of the exacerbated nationalism that prevails in most countries today. Italian fascism was an intensely nationalistic political movement, and yet it contained no elements of anti-Semitism prior to

1938; and the anti-Jewish measures later enforced as a gesture of obedience to Hitler struck no responsive chord in the Italian masses. There are many other nationalist movements both in Europe and America which have not subscribed to, and in some cases have actively protested against, anti-Semitism.

The Jewish minority has been exposed to far more than the normal share of contempt and hostility. They have represented for most peoples the very essence of foreignness, partly because they have had no country of their own to turn to or return to, and partly too because they are considered eternal exiles. This sociological anomaly of being a people without a country has created a strange and disturbing impression expressed in the legend of the Wandering Jew. There can be no doubt that this mysterious personage has symbolized the typical Jew for a great many people in the past and even in our day.

II. Economic Factors

There are four chief motivations of economic anti-Semitism:

1. The hatred and envy which is always engendered by competition in any profession, but particularly in the economic field.

2. Resentment of economically exploited groups against the economically powerful.

3. Political manipulation of class hatred by governments or powerful interests.

4. Conscious or unconscious ambivalence toward all who possess money.

Economic factors have frequently overshadowed all others in the mind of the public, and there is a tendency to attribute all conflicts between Jews and non-Jews to them alone. Jews have been regarded as the leading capitalists—even as the inventors of capitalism. This opinion has fostered one of the delusional forms of modern anti-Semitism.

Briefly, the actual historical facts are as follows:

The Jews of Palestine were for many centuries an agricultural people (the word "merchant" in Hebrew means "canaanite"). Throughout the period of classical antiquity commerce was mainly in the hands of the Greeks and Phoenicians. And when later the Jews began to engage in commerce their economic status was in no way comparable to the importance they were later to achieve.

Parkes points out that in the documents which have come down to us from this period there is not a single reference to the status of the Jews in the economic system of the times. There is no mention of wealth or power which would elicit envy and enmity among their contemporaries. It would seem that they constituted neither a menace nor a problem, but formed a normal part of society. There was of course economic rivalry between Greeks and Jews, but the competition was normal.

The war against Rome, 66–70 A.D., marked a turning point in the economic activities of the Jews. The impoverishment of Palestine, the loss of several hundred thousand young Jews, and the increase in migration toward Mesopotamia or the west, made great inroads upon the Jewish population of Palestine, and by the end of the fifth century it had virtually ceased to exist. This development led to a shift in the distribution of economic activities among the European Jews. There was a sharp decline in the number of farmers and a corresponding influx into the cities. The abandonment of farming can be explained in terms of economics—immigrants into an already fully populated country rarely find available land, and drift more easily into employment in the cities.

There is also the primordial factor of the deep psychological link between a man and his land. After the fall of Jerusalem the Jews were cut off from their native land. But Palestine was more than their homeland. It was also the focal center of their religion. So that in clinging to their religious faith, the medieval Jews also kept alive and active the ties which bound them to their native land, lost centuries before. These psychological factors played no small part in the reluctance of the Jews to become farmers in a foreign country. We have only to consider the enthusiasm and competence with which the young Jews of Palestine have thrown themselves into the business of farming after centuries of urban life to realize the tremendous importance of the psychological relationship between man and the soil he cultivates.

The second change in their economic status was the result of a long process. Historians link it to the introduction of the canonical laws of the Catholic Church into the legislation of the Christian Roman emperors of the fourth century. From then on there occurred a gradual breakdown of Jewish political and economic equality, which became total some centuries later when, after the fall of the Roman Empire, because they were not Christians, they were relegated to an inferior status.

But even after that, and as late as the eleventh century, there were still Jewish farmers, merchants, craftsmen, jewellers, goldsmiths, physicians, etc. However, a sharp turn for the worse occurred in the ninth and tenth centuries, and little by little they were excluded from all activities except commerce, tax collection and banking, and "forced to enrich themselves."*

Moneylending and usury had been forbidden in the Old Testament. The Catholic Church took over this prohibition and forbade its members to engage in moneylending. It did not, however, extend this ban to the Jews. The Rabbis were at first uncertain how to interpret the Law, but they finally decided that lending money to Gentiles was permissible; thus the Jews were able to survive economically.

Several theories have been advanced to explain Jewish economic survival and enrichment during this period. Baron attributes it to the fact that the Jews possessed in their Talmud a whole heritage of juridical and economic knowledge collected from antique civilization and from the semicapitalist society of the Roman Empire. After the fall of the Roman Empire, living as they did in the midst of peoples of lower cultural and economic levels, they easily attained a place of pre-eminence in commerce. They were further fitted for their function because they had maintained closer contacts with the Near East, through their fellow Jews, and because of their common language they were able to carry on commerce on an international level.

Another theory, that of Feiwel, is that because of

* Cf. E. Renan: *Discours et Conférences*. Paris: Calmann-Lévy, 1922.

their continual expansion from East to West via the ancient trade routes, the Jews gradually came to fulfill a vital function in the medieval world. Their banking and credit operations, which extended far beyond the countries they inhabited, created a network of exchange and fluidity of wealth throughout the civilized world. They became the operators of a sort of primitive commercial imperialism. In spite of—perhaps because of—the invaluable services the Jews rendered during this period of disintegration of the Roman world and birth pangs of the modern era, the importance they attained as the possessors and intermediaries of wealth aroused considerable jealousy and animosity. And as power gradually became centralized during the later Middle Ages, the commercial privileges and moneylending rights granted them by Charlemagne and William the Conqueror placed them in the odious light of usurers. It was natural, too, that the people who bore the brunt of the excessive spending of the rulers should blame the money handlers for their plight. Thus the princes succeeded in diverting to the Jews all the bitterness and resentment of the humble folk they were exploiting. They even went so far as to countenance dispossession and massacre of the moneylenders. It was a convenient way to get rid of their own obligations to them. Philip the Fair was particularly adroit at this type of double-dealing.

All historians are agreed on the primordial importance of these factors in the persecution and massacres of the later Middle Ages. As one chronicler put it, "the real poison which killed the Jews was their gold."

Their financially predominant position was not

of long duration; it lasted only about a hundred years. Jewish usurers were gradually supplanted by Christians, chiefly Lombardians, who soon left them far behind in the financial field. They exploited the people just as much, if not more, than the Jews had done, but profited from the prevalent custom of blaming the Jews to divert resentment away from their own malpractices, and at the same time to weaken Jewish competition, which still had to be reckoned with. It was then that the word "Jew" became the appellation of anyone in the money trade. Christian usurers were called "Christian Jews."

Apart from their tremendous influence on the economic development of Europe, the Jews played a significant role in another far more important sphere. The Jewish communities scattered throughout the Roman Empire and in Mesopotamia managed to survive after the fall of the Empire, and western civilization owes much to their survival, quite apart from the influence of the Jewish religion on Islam and Christianity. In the Saracen Empire, the Jews of Alexandria and Mesopotamia initiated the Arabs into the Hellenic culture, and later it was the Jews who helped to transmit the double heritage of Greek and Arabic civilizations to the peoples of medieval Europe. The Jews were philosophers, physicians, mathematicians, cartographers, navigators, poets, writers, kings' councilors. Their influence on the progress of humanity was profound. We need only mention two of the most famous Jews of that time: Avicebron—or Ibn Gabirol, as he was known in Arabic—the founder of scholastic philosophy, and Maimonides, the famous philosopher and physician of the thirteenth century.

By the beginning of the modern era the Jews had lost most of their economic power and prestige except in Poland where they constituted the only middle class between the nobles and the peasants. Later, not only in Central Europe but also in certain communities of Western Europe, the Jews again began to take an interest in the game of finance and in the new conditions governing it, bringing to bear all their traditional knowledge and their spirit of enterprise. In the eighteenth century some of them had escaped from the moral bonds of the ghetto and begun to take an active part in the economic affairs of Europe, just as before them other Jews had freed themselves from the intellectual ghetto and plunged into the mainstream of contemporary philosophy. We might mention Spinoza, the great seventeenth century philosopher. Montaigne, also, by the Nurenberg laws, should be considered a Jew.

Israel, therefore, re-entered the life of nations through economic and intellectual gates, and it is interesting to note that the philosophers preceded the bankers. It was a rapid and comprehensive re-entry. Nevertheless there was a fundamental difference between the status of the Jews in the world economy of the Middle Ages and in that of the nineteenth and twentieth centuries. In the Middle Ages, they constituted within each nation a kind of foreign capitalist organization whose hegemony extended all over Europe, whereas in the nineteenth century the majority of European Jews were to be found in the middle classes, and relatively few were big capitalists.

Feiwel divides their recent economic history into two diametrically opposite periods, the first period—

up to 1860–1870—corresponding to the rise of the middle classes and the second to their subsequent decline. Indeed between 1850 and 1870 which was a period of optimism and capitalist expansion, one might have assumed that total assimilation was only a matter of time and that the ancient prejudices against Jews would gradually lose their *raison d'être*. And if all Jews had been like the western Jews this might very probably have happened. But in the background there were the oppressed, impoverished masses of Russian Jews.

In the Middle Ages the Catholic Church and the princes and Christian bankers had taken advantage of anti-Jewish sentiment to seize Jewish capital. In modern times the coveting of Jewish wealth has been no negligible factor in the adoption of anti-Semitic policies.

According to Horkheimer, there is a tendency in modern economics to dispense with the function of the intermediary—to eliminate the "sphere of distribution" which is between the "sphere of production" and the "sphere of consumption." Since a considerable proportion of Jews have been active in the sphere of distribution, this tendency has undoubtedly sharpened competition and intensified anti-Semitism among Gentiles in the same sphere of activity. This was an important factor in anti-Semitism in Germany between the two World Wars.*

The rising tide of anti-Semitism in Poland during that same period was also economically determined

---

* The majority of Nazi party members was recruited from among the middle classes, "proletarianized" during the economic chaos that followed defeat.

and can be traced to the disorganization and disintegration of that part of Europe as a result of the Treaty of Versailles. In Poland there was the additional factor of the recent rise of the non-Jewish middle class. Naturally they entered into competition with the Jews who had previously held undisputed control of the middle-class functions.

The liberal professions also fall into the sphere of distribution, where competition between Jews and Gentiles, and its concomitant—anti-Semitism—have intensified. It is interesting to note that in countries in full expansion the Jews were assimilated without difficulty, but in impoverished countries like Austria and Russia before 1914, and in Germany after 1918, competition was so fierce that the concentration of Jews in the liberal professions was bound to cause increased tension and friction.*

In the long run, any "intermediary" role becomes a thankless one. An intermediary is used just so long as his services are necessary. When he is no longer needed he is ruthlessly discarded. He will be indignantly criti-

* Let me take as an example of these causes of friction the one of which I am best qualified to speak: namely, the concentration of so many foreign Jews in the medical profession in France, which was undoubtedly partially responsible for the marked anti-Semitism current in French medical circles. The story, as told me by the late Dr. Henri Codet, is worth telling. In 1930 the French Government removed many of the obstacles in the path of foreigners trying to obtain licenses to practice medicine in France. As a result many Jews who were having a hard time practicing in their own countries (Poland and Roumania, for example), chose to practice in France, and there was a considerable influx of Jewish doctors in and around Paris. A delegation of French doctors complained to the government of this competition and received the following explanation: A plan to create a surplus of foreign doctors had been initiated by M. Loucheur, Minister of Labor at the time. His ultimate aim was to socialize medicine and he had conceived the idea of forming a group of foreign doctors who would be more amenable to the idea than their French colleagues.

cized if he persists in claiming his "percentage" in transactions where he is now superfluous. This indignation is the stronger if the intermediary is a foreigner, and strongest of all if he is a Jew. Then the hostility, actually based on economic interest, takes on the character of moral indignation.

There is also quite another set of motivations, stemming from the symbolic significance in man's unconscious of money and wealth.* Psychoanalysis has shown that in the unconscious money is curiously and inexplicably associated with feces. During one stage of development the child exhibits a predominant interest in his excrementary functions. During the same stage he manifests reactions of cruelty toward the people in his environment. The fact that these two tendencies coexist in the same stage explains why cupidity is associated with cruelty in man's mind. Shylock, in fact, represents the two vices traditionally imputed to the Jews. The possession of money arouses contradictory reactions in the human psyche: admiration and envy, but also hatred and disgust. The curse on riches is an old one. It predates our capitalist era by many centuries.

There is also the factor of the "cultural lag" (W. F. Ogburn) in a society at any point in its economic development. Remnants of feudal ideologies still persist in the face of modern economic and technological progress. These have given rise to the hypocritical attitude towards money and money matters that is so typical of European anti-Semites, who make use of the mechanisms of displacement and projection to blame the Jews for all the social problems the capitalist sys-

---

* "The Jews bear first the curse of blood and then the curse of gold" (Marie Bonaparte).

tem has brought in its wake. On the other hand, in countries like the United States, where there are fewer traces of feudal thinking and where interest in money matters can be frankly and openly expressed, the same displacement mechanism may be detected in the reproaches of sharp practice brought against the Jews.

There is one other reason for the close relationship between economic factors and phenomena of group psychology and in particular of group aggression. It is obvious that these economic factors come within the frame of reference of the drives for self-preservation. It is well known that aggression is the usual reaction to frustration or menace. The same reaction is aroused under threat of deprivation of property. For property is unconsciously identified with the self, as a kind of extension of the self. Thus all our possessions—land, house, money, etc.—are psychologically a part of our person. Any threat to this extension of ourselves stimulates immediate aggressive reactions. The average man is completely ignorant of the laws which govern economics. He feels helpless when unforeseen events threaten his security or when he finds himself held down in a position of inferiority without hope of betterment. Almost inevitably he reacts violently, if mistakenly, against the Jews, whom folklore and tradition have always represented as the authors and exploiters of human misery.

III. Religious Fanaticism

Religious anti-Semitism ranks with xenophobia as one of the oldest forms of anti-Semitism, and by many it has been considered by far the most significant. It is of course just one manifestation of the phenomenon of intolerance common to most, if not all, religions.

There seems to be a difference between polytheisms and monotheisms in this respect. Although there are some well-known instances of intolerance in polytheistic religions, on the whole they have shown more tolerance than monotheisms. They imposed their gods on their defeated enemies, but quite often they tolerated the gods of the conquered people alongside their own, sometimes even incorporating them into their pantheons.

In the case of the monotheistic religions it is quite a different story. Judaism, Catholicism, Greek or Russian Orthodoxy, and Islam, without exception refused to tolerate a rival religion in their midst when they had the power to persecute it. Toynbee has observed that the concept of a universal God seems to be inseparable from the concept of a jealous and intolerant God.

The reciprocal restrictions imposed by Catholics and Protestants in countries where they have coexisted are so very similar to the restrictions imposed on Jews that it is impossible not to see the connection. Renan was struck by the similarity of the accusations made against both Jews and Protestants by the French Catholics. And in countries where the Protestants are in the majority the same faults are attributed to Catholics and Jews.*

When writers refer to religious anti-Semitism, however, they do not mean this general form of religious intolerance. They mean the type of religious

---

* It is also interesting that the early Christians were accused of the practice of ritual murder by the Romans long before the Jews were similarly accused, and that later certain heretical groups were accused of the same crime by the Catholics.

RELIGIOUS FANATICISM

anti-Semitism that has left an indelible imprint on the thinking of modern man by implanting in his mind the mythical image of the accursed Jew. This type, which may be termed pathological, has its historical roots in the schism between Judaism and Christianity. It might be useful here to review briefly the history of that event.

For several centuries before the teachings of Christ there had been a conflict in Judaism between two elements variously described by historians as "provincialism and universalism" (Toynbee), and "nationalism and universalism" (Foot Moore). This conflict represented the gradual evolution of the concepts of Jehovah from a tribal god to the God of the Universe. The universalist tendencies found their most forceful expression in Pharisaism, and culminated in the "Testament of the Twelve Patriarchs," in the writings of Philo of Alexandria, in the teachings of Hillel the Great and his descendants, the Rabbis, who wrote the Talmud, as well as in the teachings of Jesus.

> Precisely when Judaism seemed to be nearing the goal of its history—the reconciliation of its national and universal ideologies, through a process of inner and outer growth as an ethnico-religious unity beyond the bounds of state and territory—it suffered a sudden reverse. . . . The rise of Christianity, and its separation from Judaism, as well as the destruction of the Second Temple which greatly facilitated it, checked the great expansion of the Jewish people. One of the most remarkable movements of all times thus came to an abrupt end (Baron).

As regards the new sect which sprang up within Judaism and later became Christianity, most modern authors agree that it is the outcome of a syncretization of Jewish religious ideas with Greek philosophical theories, with the addition of concepts taken from oriental cults of non-Jewish origin.

> It was among the Jews and on Jewish soil that Jesus was born; it was to the Jews that he preached, and to the Jews alone. In its first beginnings, Christianity was a Jewish phenomenon (Guignebert).

The first Christians were all Jews, or Greeks practicing the Jewish religion.

Bertrand Russell points out the striking similarity between the teachings of Jesus and of St. Paul on the one hand, and the teachings of the Pharisees as contained in the Testament of the Twelve Patriarchs. Renan, Klausner and Foot Moore have compared them to the ethical principles of the Rabbis as set down in the part of the Talmud called Pirke Aboth. Jesus' denunciation of the bigotry and hypocrisy of the Pharisees has its counterpart in the Talmud written by these very Pharisees.

Not only has their Bible remained the Sacred Book for the Christian Church, but also the liturgical offices, religious rites and customs of the Jews have had a profound influence on the ordering of the Christian life. Nevertheless, though it is true that Christianity issued from Judaism, it is also true that its real source of inspiration was the Hellenist Judaism of the Diaspora, established on Greek soil and permeated with Greek culture.

The great schism between Judaism and Christianity came about very gradually. The foundations for the Christian Church were being laid even before the destruction of the Temple. Saul of Tarsus, the Apostle Paul, was the founder. In his attempt to expand Judaism, as he understood it, he went beyond it and created a new religion.

The destruction of the Temple and the resulting loss of power and prestige of Palestinian Judaism in the eyes of the hellenized Jews increased the separatist tendencies of the new sect which was to become Christianity. These separatist tendencies were further strengthened as a result of the suppression of the revolt of Bar Kocheba and the subsequent reprisals. During the revolts against Rome, Jews and Judaeo-Christians accused each other of lack of patriotism and treason. By the end of the second century the schism was virtually complete. According to Baron, the Gospels were rewritten in this period with a strongly anti-Jewish bias and incorporated in their new form in the New Testament. Animosity against the Jews was inevitably heightened during the persecutions of the Christians by Rome during the third century, when Christianity was declared illegal, while Judaism remained a *religio licita*.

Others have seen the separation of Christianity from its parent religion as an element in the struggle of the Greco-Roman world against the threat of oriental expansion. Jewish traditional rites and ceremonies were gradually discarded and the young Christian religion was given an orientation that restored the prestige of Greco-Roman culture.

> Roman Catholicism became the heir of Imperial Rome (Toynbee).

Others again interpret the rise of Christianity as a manifestation of the revolt of the impoverished Palestinian proletariat against Rome and the upper- and middle-class Jews—the Sadduccees and the Pharisees. According to this view one section of the proletariat fought it out in the political and military sphere, while the Christians expressed their revolt by clinging to their hope for the imminent coming of the apocalyptic Age and the destruction of the hated Roman Empire.

But whatever the original causes of this ever-widening schism, the outcome was that at the end of several centuries two distinct and rival religions emerged, both bent on conquest of the Roman world, so that it was inevitable that they should clash. Christianity was in the embarrassing situation of owing its very existence to its rival. Judaism still enjoyed tremendous prestige, in spite of its diminishing power, and so constituted a real threat. It was necessary for the Christians to prove that ancient Israel had lost favor in the sight of God and that Christianity was the true Israel, the favorite son of God. This blend of attachment and obligation to Judaism, on the one hand, and of resentment and revolt, on the other—in other words, this ambivalence—has been typical of the Christian attitude toward Judaism from the beginning of its history.

Ambivalence then (as well as other profound but unconscious motivations) explains the anti-Jewish tenor of the writings of the Fathers of the Church, to which Parkes traces the roots of the modern form of anti-Semitism. The work of exegesis undertaken by the Church Fathers reinterpreted the Old Testament and presented the history of the Jewish people in two phases, before and after the Incarnation; the refusal of the Jews to believe in Jesus Christ caused them to be rejected by God; all that had been pleasing to God was attributed to the New Israel; all that had provoked God to anger, to ancient Israel. The Christian Fathers represented the Jews as traitors to God and repudiated by him. In this they were motivated not so much by hatred of the Jews as by the historical necessity of establishing Christianity as a religion in its own right, independent of the parent religion. On a less conscious level their writings represent the efforts of the newly emancipated Christian Church to retain the prestige of the ancient and venerable traditions of Judaism, and perhaps also to acknowledge its debt to the Jews,

> . . . since through their fall salvation is come unto the Gentiles (Romans: XI:ii).

Thus we find from the beginning a dual attitude toward the Jews: violence and bitter denunciation, on the one hand, and on the other, a special tolerance in the very heart of the Church, because Christianity was

> . . . a branch that had sprung from the tree of Judah (Paul).

Among individual Christians these special, contradictory reactions are based psychologically on the feelings every son experiences toward his father. He owes him his very existence, but unconsciously regards him as a rival and seeks to emancipate himself as he grows older. So we see that there is a parallel between the early struggles of the Christian Church and its final emergence as an independent religion, and the psychological evolution of succeeding generations of individual Christians.

Historically, the stages in Judaeo-Christian relations during the first millenium can be divided into three phases: the first phase up to the destruction of the Jewish State, the second phase up to the emergence of Catholic Christianity armed with secular power and therefore potentially able to impose its will, and the third phase in which the Church's potential power was converted into effective power.

The second phase began when Christianity became the official religion of the Roman Empire. Up to that time Judaism had been a licit religion on the same footing as other religions within the Empire, but thereafter it came under the legal pressure of the canonical laws. Nevertheless, no matter how severely hampered and weakened by these laws, Judaism found protection under them and continued to survive.

The third phase began with the formation in Western Europe of an increasing number of nations under the dominance of the Catholic Church. We saw that during the centuries which followed the conquest of Rome by the barbarians and the gradual disintegration of the Roman Empire, the Jews by slow degrees lost their Roman citizenship and became the personal property of the princes who accorded them protection. Their legal and economic status deteriorated during the Middle Ages until they came to be considered inferior to other men, more akin to beasts.

The progressive Christianization of the peoples of Europe, the growing influence of the Church over the rulers of the various states, and the fanaticism of the recently converted semi-barbarian masses, all provided pretexts for brutal mistreatment of the Jews. The first pogrom took place in 1096, at the time of the First Crusade. For several centuries thereafter the Jews were subjected to bullying, expulsion, pillage, massacre and forced conversion. But religious fanaticism was not by any means the only driving force—hatred of the usurers had already become an important motivation.

Lasserre has observed that the Catholic Church, in its triumphant march toward the spiritual unification of the world, was mortified that among all the cults that had flourished in the Roman Empire, only the Synagogue had been able to withstand Christian propaganda. The only obstacle in the path of the Christians toward religious supremacy was this handful of Jews "stubbornly entrenched in their satanic blindness." It is not surprising that the Church yielded to the temptation of using its secular power and influence with the princes to reduce these stubborn, unyielding unbelievers to a state of pariahdom on the fringes of society.

A distinction must be drawn, however, between the attitude of the Papacy and that of the lower clergy. The Papacy was on the whole much less hostile, and maintained in principle the attitude of genuine ambivalence that had developed out of the original schism.

The official attitude of the Church had been defined by Pope Gregory the Great (590–604) in his *Constitutio pro Judeis*, wherein he established the principles protecting the religious practices of the Jews within the strict limits of the Law. The thirteenth century Popes reaffirmed the principles of Gregory I but emphasized the more hostile aspects of his pronouncements. Pope Innocent III (1198–1216) defined the theological position of the Jews in the Christian world thus:

> The Jews' guilt of the crucifixion of Jesus consigned them to perpetual servitude, and, like Cain, they are to be wanderers and fugitives . . . the Jews will not dare to

raise their necks, bowed under the yoke of perpetual slavery, against the reverence of the Christian faith.

And yet these same thirteenth century Popes appealed to Christian charity to protect the Jews from excessive persecution. The theological reasons adduced for this protection were that the Jews were witnesses of the true Christian faith; their very existence was proof of the Gospels and their abasement proof of the triumph of Christianity. They were still the Guardians of the Scriptures, and according to a prophecy contained in the book of Isaiah and according to St. Paul, a remnant of Israel would be saved and the second coming of Christ would depend on the conversion of these survivors. Therefore, though the Jews might be oppressed, they must not be exterminated—another example of the strange paradox of tolerance and hatred which has always characterized Christian ambivalence toward Judaism.

Thus the process of separation between Judaism and Christianity had psychological and historical repercussions on medieval Christians, and these repercussions have continued to affect people raised in the Christian faith to this day. We have seen the parallel between the struggle of the young religion against the parent religion and the unconscious personal struggle of every man against his father. The important role of the oedipus complex in the development of the individual illuminates the conflicts between the religion in which God the Father is supreme and the religion in which the Son, while not actually supplanting the Father, yet holds an equal place with him, and in which the Mother is closer to the Son than to the Father.

Religious anti-Semitism is an expression of the intolerance inherent in monotheistic religions. It is also a demonstration of the amount of cruelty that can be perpetrated in the name of the highest principles of love and charity. The explanation of such cruelty is to be found in the ambivalence of all human emotions and especially in those of a child toward his father and —by extension—those of a believer toward his God. Anyone who does not share his faith is an object of hatred. Monotheists are all the more intolerant of unbelievers because their one and only God will not tolerate any ambivalence in their feelings toward him. He demands absolute submission and unquestioning devotion to the ethical principles established in his name. We have seen that these demands are projections into the universe of the father figure, of the father-son relationship and of the superego—the heir to the oedipus complex. Whatever remains of the inevitable ambivalence toward the father and his substitutes, and of revolt against the moral exigencies of religion, creates in the devout monotheist unconscious rebellion and ambivalence toward his God. These feelings are generally either repressed or revealed only indirectly—as for example in the religious doubts which assail many believers at certain moments in their lives.*

The measure of a believer's hatred of an unbeliever, therefore, is the measure of his own unconscious struggle to repress ambivalent feelings toward his God. The Christian attitude toward Jews is still further complicated by the fact of the common origin of Juda-

---

* It is also significant that the Jews are regarded as the living proof of the authenticity of Gospel history—as if this history needed confirmation in the minds of devout Christians.

ism and Christianity, of their subsequent separation, and of the dual and contradictory concept of the Jew in Christian theology.

Most monotheistic religions evolve a concept which is the antithesis of their God. They create a principle of evil—the Devil. The Devil may have the features of a foreign deity or of a fallen deity. Through the teachings of the Christian Fathers, Christians came to identify the Jews with the Devil, and to consider them the incarnation of Evil. Christians of simple faith still tend to recall only those archaic aspects of the God of the Jews which are the most akin to the spirit of Evil: his anger and vindictiveness. They tend to forget that the Jewish religion has mellowed during the course of the ensuing centuries to a point where the ethics of Judaism are similar to Christian ethics.

The Christian sees the Jew in this diabolical light because the Devil represents his own "inner enemy." He is also motivated by other factors stemming from the origins of Christianity. The Jews had been the Chosen People. Christians are taught that God abandoned the Jews and transferred all His love and solicitude to the Christians. Yet the continued existence of the Jews, and especially of prosperous and successful Jews, seems like a denial of this promise and consequently like a challenge to the Christian faith. From time to time Christians take things into their own hands, and despoil and kill Jews in the name of God in order to prove to the Jews and to themselves that God has in very truth forsaken them. Here we have another illustration of the interplay of religious and economic factors in the dynamics of anti-Semitism.

There have been various attempts to explain why

anti-Semitism should have flared up so violently toward the end of the eleventh century, when the pogroms began. One theory is that the Christianization of semi-barbarian peoples of Europe was of too recent a date for the new religion to have brought any appreciable amelioration in their customs. Freud has suggested that the flare-up may have been due to fanaticism resulting from the intense ambivalence of the European peoples toward the new religion so recently, and sometimes even forcibly, adopted. Another theory is that during this period of formation of new nations the Jews were becoming increasingly alien to the native populations at the same time that their economic role was becoming increasingly unpopular. Still another theory attributes the increase in anti-Semitism at that time to the fact that the number of Christians capable of filling the Jewish economic functions was progressively increasing, with the result that the Jews were becoming less indispensable to the princes and to the Church, who gradually withdrew their protection.

The Jews undoubtedly owe their survival through these centuries of hardship and oppression to their heroic devotion to their religious faith. Nevertheless, living as they were in isolated and scattered communities throughout Europe, they would have been powerless to resist had the Catholic Church set out to exterminate them along with the Christian heretical sects. The Jews, however, were never considered heretics; they were the only non-Christian group tolerated on Christian soil.

Three centuries later the Protestants did not prove much more tolerant toward the Jews than the Catholics had been. Luther began by inviting them to join the new religious movement, but after their refusal he fulminated against them. Indirectly, however, the Protestants helped to abate the tide of anti-Semitism by reviving general interest in the Hebrew language, which led to a fuller knowledge and appreciation of Judaism. But the change for the better in the general attitude toward Jews which began in that period was chiefly due to the growth of humanism, to the intellectual and philosophical movements which developed in Europe after the Renaissance, and finally, to the radical political and social changes which followed the French and American Revolutions.

In our day it would seem that religion plays a diminishing role in the destiny of western civilization, and a negative one in the "malady of the modern world" of which Nazism was a symptom. In fact, much of the malaise from which modern man suffers might be attributed to the gradual disintegration of his religious faith. It is strange, therefore, that there are people today who, out of their whole religious heritage, have retained only the prejudices. Anti-Semitism in their case becomes a sort of caricature of their lost faith.

IV. Anti-Christianism

National Socialism has been described as a kind of religion. As a religion, however, it had nothing in common with Christianity. It was, in fact, anti-Christian. Maritain has compared the struggle of National Socialism against the democracies to the struggle of the pagan states against Christianity. Here is what the official theorist of the *Deutschreligion*, Professor Ernst Bergmann, had to say:

The period of world religion draws to its close. A people which returns to race and soil, which has recognized the world peril of international Judaism, can no longer tolerate in its churches a religion which calls the sacred writings of the Jews its "Gospel." Germania's reconstruction would be wrecked by this inner untruth . . . That is why the watchword of the German religion is: Away from Rome and Jerusalem!*

There are many points of resemblance between Nazi anti-Semitism and medieval anti-Semitism. This is not surprising since the Nazi leaders had been raised in the Christian tradition in which all the elements of anti-Semitism are implicit. And as the Christian fanatic regarded the existence of an unbeliever as an offence against God, so the Nazis regarded the existence of the Jews as an insult to the Aryan race. According to the dogma of the new race religion, Aryan blood must be purged of the impurities introduced by an admixture of Jewish blood in order that the German race might be freed of any taint of weakness. The whole weight of the aggression of a militant religion was thus directed against the Jews in the Nazi race religion.

But side by side with these analogies with medieval anti-Semitism, which are signs of historic continuity, there are also differences. And it is the differences that are fundamentally important for an understanding of the phenomenon of Nazi anti-Semitism.

In the previous chapter we said that the function of anti-Semitism in the Middle Ages was to preserve the Christian faith, whereas the function of Nazi anti-Semitism was to destroy it. National Socialism is anti-Christian not only because of its pagan elements, but

* *Die Thesen der Deutschreligion* (Quoted by Baron).

also because of its deification of State and Race. In its essentials it is an attack on the very foundations of Christianity. Freud first stressed that Nazi anti-Semitism was disguised anti-Christianism. He also pointed out that history shows that it is always the more recent and unwilling converts to Christianity who have been the most intensely anti-Semitic.

The open and avowed aim of Hitler was to root out forever from the German mind any attachments or preoccupations which did not exclusively serve the interests of the German State and the Master Race. He set himself to break down and nullify the heritage of a thousand years of civilization; to destroy the principles of law inherited from Rome, the principles of truth and beauty inherited from Greece, and of freedom, justice, charity and human dignity inherited from Judaism and Christianity.

What is the psychoanalytic interpretation of these ideals and principles? In the structural scheme of the human psyche which we have adopted from Freud, ethical principles derive from the superego. Their formulation and their integration into a religious system represents primarily man's recognition of the superego forces, and secondly, their elaboration by the conscious ego which endows them with universal dignity and worth. For the religious man, basic moral laws are given by God, and all men should obey them. For the psychoanalyst regarding these laws from the point of view of their human and social origin, they have a universal value, since all men have a superego.

Civilization owes its development to the gradually increasing control of the superego and of the ego over the instinctual drives: in other words, progress is achieved at the expense of the instinctual drives. The process results in a change in the economy of the drives which Freud has compared to the domestication of animals.

The Nazi "revolution," and the totalitarian state, which Hitler tried to impose on humanity, was in effect a revolt of the instinctual drives against the universally accepted forces of the superego. In his attempt to build a Master Race, Hitler tried to eradicate the superego because it generates moral conscience and inhibits aggression. Basic laws of morality had no intrinsic value for the Nazis unless they could be made to serve the interests of the Master Race and of the Führer. Ethical values were entirely subordinated to interest and expediency.

The anti-Christianism of the Nazis, disguised as anti-Semitism, was one aspect of their revolt against the forces of the superego. Their anti-Semitism was directly descended from medieval Christian anti-Semitism: the same symbols were used and the same emotions involved. But its function had changed (Heinz Hartmann).

For Christians the function of anti-Semitism has been that of a displacement and projection of their unconscious revolt against Christ, while keeping their love for Christ intact on a conscious level. For the anti-Christian Nazis, the revolt against Christ and the superego he represents was a conscious one, though it might still be denied and camouflaged. Christ, symbol of moral force, giving his life for the salvation of humanity, was no longer an acceptable ideal for the followers of Hitler. On the contrary, Christ was more identified with Israel—source of Christian morality. Jews symbolized for the Nazis the ultimate victory of right over might. Conscience was the only force that might prevent the German people from becoming ideal Nazis—that is to say, perfect human machines devoid of scruples and moral sense. And so, beyond Israel, the Jews symbolized Christianity and Christ. The Nazis did not dare to attack Christianity too openly; instead they destroyed its double—Judaism. They imposed the destiny of Christ on the Jews, sacrificing them in an unconscious effort to rid themselves on this scapegoat of their guilt and remorse.

Chapter IV

I. JEWISH CHARACTER TRAITS

I

How is it that throughout the centuries Jews have represented so many and such different ideas for anti-Semites? Why have they always been considered different from other men? Are they really different? Is there any basis for the many reproaches heaped upon them? Have they any special personality traits which foster this dislike and animosity?

Some of the accusations brought against them are so fantastic that it may seem insulting to the memory of the victims of anti-Semitism to ask the question. But since it is our intention to maintain an objective and impartial attitude throughout this book, all aspects of the problem must be taken up one by one and an attempt made to understand them.

When a psychoanalyst has a patient who complains of continual conflicts with his fellows, he can be fairly certain that there are some traits or patterns of behavior in the patient's own personality make-up which provoke these conflicts. Are we justified in applying this diagnosis of an individual type of patient to a group, and in concluding that the almost universal prevalence of hostility toward Jews presupposes the existence of something in the psychological make-up of the Jew that fosters it?

When such symptoms occur in a patient, psychoanalysis affords a means of tracing them back to their origins in some underlying personality disturbance. Sometimes they can be traced to the influence of unsuccessfully repressed tendencies trying by indirect means to break through into overt behavior, either in the form of an inhibiting effect on the patient's activity, or as stereotyped reactions, quite unadapted to the adult situation. Sometimes these symptoms are the work of the patient's inner anxiety or unconscious guilt feelings attracting hostility from the environment. Or again they may be due to the perseveration of affective demands which the adult environment can not satisfy. Let us limit ourselves to a consideration of these few patterns of neurosis, common to the clinical experience of every psychoanalyst.

In the course of a prolonged period of therapy the psychoanalyst is usually able to determine the part which the patient's mind has played in these conflicts with his environment. He can detect the forces in play and the psychological mechanisms that allow them to break through. Furthermore, he is generally able to estimate with a fair degree of accuracy the average reactions to be expected from the environment to this particular type of person.

One would be tempted to hope that by applying the criteria and methods used in psychoanalysis of individual cases to collective groups we might find the key to the problem that here concerns us—the problem of the interreactions of Jews and non-Jews. Unfortunately, such a transposition of method on a wholesale scale is not feasible.

It is true that the psychoanalyst can study the conflicts of a Jewish patient with his non-Jewish fellow men, from the point of view of his individual behavior and of their reactions to him as a Jew. But he cannot ascertain why the non-Jewish environment reacts as it does toward Jews in general, nor whether the special traits of the patient are to be attributed to the fact that he is a Jew. All he can establish is that certain traits in his patient are considered Jewish traits.

It cannot be too heavily emphasized that there is no question here of any fundamental differences between Jews and other members of the human family. What are often considered specifically Jewish traits turn out upon closer examination to be traits common to all mankind; actually only slight differences in degree and distribution of traits may reveal the Jew.

For instance, there are no specifically "Jewish" deviations in the evolution of the oedipus complex or of the castration complex, nor any "Jewish" mode of development of the libido. However, certain means of resolution of the oedipus complex and fixations at certain stages in the development of the libido do seem to occur more frequently among Jews than Gentiles. In our opinion, these expressions are connected with the aggressive drives. And if there is anything peculiar to the Jewish mind, it would seem to be the special ways in which the ego deals with the aggressive drives, and the defense mechanisms the Jews have elaborated in terms of the peculiar circumstances of their social environment. Thus these "Jewish traits" are largely formed under the pressure of the non-Jewish environment, which, in turn, reacts in terms of the general attitude toward Jews. They are also the outcome of the impact on a given Jew of his fellow Jews. Furthermore, both Jewish and non-Jewish reactions arise as much out of the traditional past as out of the actual situation.

Probably the best way to study Jewish characteristics, in so far as they exist at all, would be to compare a Jewish analysand with a number of other individuals who have in common with him the fact of being Jews. Next, these reactions would have to be compared with the reactions of a given number of non-Jews. And only if real differences in type, intensity and frequency of certain reactions were found, could we proceed to an analysis in depth of what are known as "Jewish traits."

Obviously the clinical observations of a single psychoanalyst are far from adequate for such a study. All we can hope to do in this book is to accumulate as much data as we can concerning the Jewish personality and character, supplementing them with our own personal observations of Jews of many different social strata and nationalities, and with opinions current about them in their own milieu.

A number of modern sociologists have directed their efforts to the study of the psychology of nations. Others have criticized these studies on the grounds that they contribute to the mythology rather than to the psychology of nations. In the case of such a heterogeneous and widely scattered group as the Jews, the sociopsychological value of this approach is particularly questionable.

Jacques Debré has pointed out another type of difficulty in attempting to define the psychology of the Jews. When all the anti-Jewish criticisms are collected into categories, the result is found to be a series of double entries, in which each epithet is paired with its opposite. They are accused of sordid avarice and ostentatious spending; of excessive individualism and exaggerated devotion to social "causes;" of lack of tact and oversubtlety; of obsequious boot-licking and ruthless egotism; of self-depreciation and arrogance.* Sometimes these self-contradictory criticisms are made by different people, but quite as often they are made by the same person more or less in the same breath. Could it be that they are really an expression of anti-Jewish feelings seeking outlet and justification? All deviations of opinion, everything that each particular faction sees as decadence or degeneracy, is blamed on the influence of the so-called Jewish mentality: liberalism, socialism, communism; capitalism, materialism; intellectuality, modern trends in literature and art. In fact, all that is disturbing in modern life tends to be blamed on the Jews; and this attitude is generally accompanied with nostalgia for "the good old days" when apparently there were no Jews.

Let us assume for the moment that this series of contradictory criticism of Jews is not the result of prejudice and ill-will, and that it has some foundation in fact. How would one set about proving such assumptions? What criteria and methods should be used to determine, for example, whether contradictory traits in the same individual are found only in Jews, or whether they are observed in both Jews and non-Jews; and if so, whether they occur more frequently or are more pronounced in Jews than in non-Jews; or whether the apparent contradiction comes from the fact that in

---

* The writer was told one day that Jews were either too well assimilated or not assimilated enough—an excellent example of this type of self-contradictory criticism.

a given group of Jews there will be found a number of individuals exhibiting one set of traits and a corresponding number exhibiting the opposite set? Before coming to any conclusions all these and many similar questions would have to be investigated in a comparative study on properly selected groups of Jewish and non-Jewish subjects.

II

Other difficulties inherent in the "national psychology" method are well illustrated in the work of three German authors, Bauer, Fischer and Lentz,* who made a detailed comparative study of Germans and Jews, as a result of which they reached the conclusion that—far from being widely divergent—there were some close parallels between the two peoples. They found, for example, that both Germans and Jews are characterized by good intellectual capacity and strong will power. According to these authors, both Germans and Jews show a marked spirit of enterprise, the Germans, however, being more prone to use force, and the Jews ruse, to attain their ends.

Now, in a juxtaposition of individual Jews and individual Germans this parallel may have some validity. But there are no valid grounds for stating that the above traits are more pronounced, or occur more frequently, among Germans and Jews than among individuals of other nations. It is important, too, to know whether the observations were made on German Jews or on Jews in general. If they were made on German

* As quoted by H. Neuville, Peuples ou Races. *Encyclopédie Francaise*, Vol. II.

Jews then the findings would be more acceptable, since Jews are known to be profoundly influenced by the peoples among whom they live. In any case the data on which the criteria for this comparative study were based are too vague.

But even if we admit for the sake of argument that these analogies between Germans and Jews have been established on an adequately scientific basis, the fact remains that in numerous other respects there are vast differences, which become especially pronounced from the standpoint of their behavior as groups.

For example, there are intense in-group antagonisms among Jews, of a kind which has no parallel in the German group. There is also a marked difference in the common aims and ideals which knit the groups together. For the Germans, the consciousness of belonging to the Reich was a powerful affective force which inspired them to great personal sacrifice in a desire to further its power and prestige. In contrast, Jews have for a long time been profoundly divided in their attitude toward Zionism and the State of Israel. Their collective idealism has been centered in their Messianic hopes and beliefs. There were two main currents in these Messianic beliefs—two interpretations of the role of the Jews in world history. The first interpretation implied strong temporal ambitions. The coming Messiah was conceived as a warrior who would crush the pagans, who would rebuild Jerusalem and the Temple, restore to the kingdom of Israel all its lost power and prestige, and give to the Jews world domination. This conception is an expression of religious imperialism. The second Messianic interpretation—and the one which has prevailed to the present epoch—was that of the Pharisees, and contained no temporal ambitions. It implied faith in the survival of the Jewish people until the coming of the Messiah. At his coming, thanks to Israel, justice will reign on earth and the Jewish people will be a shining banner for the peoples of the world.*

During the present century Zionism has brought about a rebirth of temporal aspirations among Jews. Zionism, however, is less an expression of Messianic ideals than of an urgent need for physical security.

It has been observed that there is a strong resemblance between the so-called typically German behavior traits and some of the traits commonly found in obsessional neuroses.** It is interesting that there is a similar resemblance between certain types of obsessive neurotics and devout orthodox Jews, punctilious in the observance of the rites and ceremonies of their religion. But whereas the Germans are obsessed with order, cleanliness, punctuality, the Jews are obsessed with what is pure and impure, just and unjust. Germans and Jews might be said to represent two different types of compulsive neuroses, the one based on the function of elimination and the so-called "sphincter" morality, and the other on the repression of aggression and "right" and "wrong." Both are based on the learning of acceptable behavior and both are characteristic of two types of obsessional neurosis. Could it be that both are also characteristic of the two "national" mentalities? There is not sufficient evidence for such a statement, although—in regard to the Jews at any rate—it can be

---

* This is Renan's definition of the Jewish need to dominate.
** Kecskemeti and Leites: Some Psychological Hypotheses on Nazi Germany. *Exp. Div. for the Study of War Time Communications.* Doc. 60, 1945.

said that these traits do develop frequently, particularly in connection with the building up of defense mechanisms against physical aggression.

III

In the field of sociology there have been several studies made on Jews which indirectly serve to reveal some interesting aspects of "Jewish" psychology. One of the most interesting of these is a statistical report made by Ruppin, in the period before 1914. He divides the Jews into four groups, according to the degree of their assimilation with the surrounding populations:

1. *Orthodox Jews:* the majority concentrated in Russia and segregrated in the western provinces and in Galicia. The standard of living among such Jews was low, the birth rate high, their language Yiddish or Spaniole. Most of them had hardly been touched by modern civilization. They numbered about seven million in the pre-1914 period; in other words, about half the population of world Jewry at that time.

2. *Jews of more liberal religious life:* typified by the Jews of Roumania, England and America. Their standard of living was higher, their birth rate moderate, they spoke the language of the country they lived in, and perhaps also Yiddish or Spaniole, and they had come under the influence of modern civilization. They numbered about four million.

3. *Freethinking Jews:* who had abandoned observance of the Sabbath and other Jewish rites. These were well-to-do Jews, with a low birth rate, speaking exclusively the language of the country they lived in. Except for the fact that they generally intermarried

with Jews and occasionally attended the synagogue, they were assimilated into the surrounding populations. Among them was a very small percentage of converts to Christianity. They numbered about two million.

4. *Agnostic Jews:* whose break with Judaism was complete. Their birth rate was low (15–20 per 1,000), the proportion of mixed marriages among them high (30–50 per cent), and the incidence of their conversion considerable (15–40 per 1,000). They numbered about one million.

Each of these groups supplied members to the next group—the orthodox to the liberals, the liberals to the freethinkers and the freethinkers to the agnostics. The process of assimilation varied according to the conditions prevailing in the different countries but was generally completed within the span of four generations.

Between the two World Wars, the cycle described by Ruppin, though still in operation, was modified by several new factors. First among these was the economic disintegration of the countries of Central and Eastern Europe. And after America virtually closed her frontiers to immigrants from Eastern Europe in 1921, the steady stream of America-bound immigrants was halted and diverted into a thin trickle into Western Europe and Palestine. After 1933 came the emigration of German Jews to France, England and America, followed by the Austrians and Czechs, and between 1940 and 1942 a further migration of all these, plus the French and Dutch Jews, to America. In addition, during the Hitler regime, five and a half million Jews remaining in German-occupied Europe were exterminated.

Other factors came into operation to modify the

cycle of assimilation described by Ruppin. From the beginning of the twentieth century, and particularly after the First World War, there was a noticeable change in the pattern of evolution in the Jewish communities of Eastern Europe. Abandonment of orthodoxy and access to modern civilization, together with their growing realization that they would always be faced with anti-Semitism no matter where they lived, led the younger generations of Jews away from assimilation and toward a deepening awareness of belonging to a distinct national group. The Hebrew language, modernized and restored to a place of honor, became the living language of several hundred thousand Jewish immigrants to Palestine. And these Jewish colonists, who became mainly agriculturists, have, in the process of transforming their semidesert land, been themselves transformed.

IV

In connection with these diverse, distinct and dissimilar groups of Jews, it is interesting to remember that a great many people, not necessarily anti-Semitic, are convinced that the Jews form a united, homogeneous group, that they are all more or less the same type, and that all possess what they call the "Jewish mentality." This somewhat naive belief has played an important part in creating the mythical concept of "the Jew." But those who have studied the question seriously have found no such uniformity. They have found that the Jewish character offers the same range and diversity of traits, the same capacities for good and evil, as that of any other people of Europe or America.

Indeed, it has been observed that the internal strife and dissensions that exist within Jewish groups are particularly intense. Rollin* cites the articles on the Zionist Congress of Hamburg of 1909, written by the Catholic writer Angel Marvaud as special correspondent for the *Journal des Débats*.** Marvaud exploded the myth of Jewish solidarity, discipline and common ideals. He attributed the violent quarrels he witnessed not only to the extreme individualism of the Jews, but also to the fact that they have acquired the national characteristics and chauvinism of their respective countries, together with the special interests of the different classes to which they belong. In my opinion, to all these causes of dissension should be added the fact that Jews live in permanent exile.

Here is a typical example of in-group prejudice taken from a passage in Stefan Zweig, who can hardly be accused of anti-Semitism:

> In Moravia, the Jews lived in the little villages on friendly terms with the peasants and townsfolk. They showed neither the inferiority feelings nor the ceaseless opportunism which characterizes the Jews of Galicia and the East.

Incidentally, his observation carries the implication that there is a correlation between the psychological traits of the Jews and the kind of relationship they have with their non-Jewish neighbors.

Eastern European Jews are harshly judged by German Jews, but they in turn have a very poor opinion of the latter, whom they consider arrogant and full of

---

* *L'Apocalypse de Notre Temps.* Paris: Gallimard, 1936.
** One of the leading conservative newspapers in France at that time.

pretension, with German character defects superimposed on their own. French Jews would sneer at German Jews as *boches*. In addition to national antagonisms there were localized prejudices. A self-respecting Polish Jew, for example, would not have thought of giving his daughter in marriage to a Lithuanian Jew—a most contemptible creature, in his opinion. In turn, Polish Jews were despised by Russian Jews, and so on. Among American Jews the same social barriers and discriminations exist between those of German origin and those from other countries, particularly from Eastern Europe; take for example the Jewish clubs in which only Jews of German origin are admitted to membership.

Even within these various subgroups there are antagonisms. We have already mentioned those arising out of differences in social status or fortune. There are many others: orthodox Jews disapprove of their less orthodox coreligionists; nationalistic Jews despise assimilated Jews, and assimilated Jews the less well assimilated. And although it is true that in some respects they show a marked equalitarian spirit so that the humblest Jew and the most famous rabbi have a basic feeling of equality, yet side by side with this there is a form of snobbishness in claiming descent from ancient and renowned families, and disdain for those of humbler origins.

Whenever there is a wave of immigrant refugees from a neighboring country, national antagonisms among Jews are intensified. German Jews reacted with suspicious hostility toward Jews fleeing the Russian pogroms; so did the French Jews toward the German victims of Nazi persecution, and the American Jews toward refugees from Europe. Yet always, accompanying feelings of resentment against these "foreigners," sometimes so supercilious and quick to criticize the country offering them a refuge, there is a strong bond of kinship with them, and a desire to help.

V

Jewish solidarity, although greatly exaggerated by Gentiles, does nevertheless exist in two spheres. There is a religious fellowship among devout Jews of all nationalities, based on common religious practices. There is also the solidarity which emerges in times of persecution, and since this has become a more or less permanent climate for most Jews, it is now almost universal. Before 1933 persecution had not touched the lives of many except as a dim memory or a vague future threat, or at most as concern for their less fortunate brethren. But the last fifteen years have brought home the brutal realization that anti-Semitism is an imminent and dreadful menace for all Jews, in all countries and in all walks of life.

Some Jews, without ever having been persecuted themselves, have acquired all the reactions of the persecuted, through identification. A most vivid example of this suffering through identification was given by Charles Peguy, in his portrait of Bernard Lazare:*

> Here was a man who would snatch up a newspaper, and skimming rapidly through its four, six or eight pages,

---

* The well-known French journalist of the turn of the century, author of a book on the history of anti-Semitism.

would pounce on one line, and in that line would be the word "Jew." Here was a man, a seasoned newspaperman, mind you, who would grow red or turn pale at some chance phrase in a newspaper—some excerpt from an article, some cable or by-line—if this chance phrase, this cable or by-line contained the word "Jew." He had a heart that bled in every ghetto in the world; a heart that bled in Roumania and Turkey, in Russia and the Argentine, in America and Hungary; in short, wherever Jews are persecuted, which is as much as to say everywhere. Such is your Jew—a quiver of rage, and it is because of an outrage committed in the Dnieper valley. A creature in a state of perpetual tension, bearing the weight of a whole race, a whole world, on his shoulders—fifty centuries of history on his poor bowed shoulders.

This common awareness of past, present and possible future sufferings is certainly one of the strongest bonds uniting the Jews of the world. But identification with his fellow Jews is not by any means always a "voluntary" process, and the factors which have created it have also stimulated defense reactions against it.

VI

It would be interesting to make a study to find out whether the fact of always being put in the same boat and tarred with the same brush by Gentiles has led to the formation of some character traits and behavior patterns common to all Jews. Such a study might be set up on the following lines:

1. Evaluation of the social structures of selected groups, their distinctive features, institutions, important achievements.

2. Incidence of certain patterns of personality and behavior among members of the group and of atti-

tudes toward each other, toward outsiders, and toward certain ideals.

3. Characteristics of individual members of the group when acting collectively.

4. Common ideals of the group and conditions under which group consciousness is achieved.

Obviously such criteria would only acquire validity when compared with similar data compiled on other properly selected groups. In other words, one would have to compare the percentage of Jews who react in a given manner in given conditions with the percentage of Catholics or Protestants, French or Germans, and so on, who react similarly under the same conditions.

So far this type of study has only been undertaken on the economic status of Jews, on their choice of profession and occupation, and on the crime rate and insanity rate among Jews. For the present, therefore, we shall have to assume provisionally the validity of criteria based on cultural and historical data, and on direct personal observations, until such time as they are either confirmed or invalidated by scientifically established data.

For example, in connection with the choice of career, it has been justly observed that there is a correlation between a profession and the type of person who exercises it. On the one hand, each profession has a distinctive influence on the psychology and behavior of its practitioners, and, on the other, it is their type of character or personality which causes certain people to gravitate toward certain professions. If this were the only factor in operation we would be forced to the conclusion that Jews show a high degree of uniformity of character, since such a high percentage of them adopt liberal and commercial professions.

According to Baron, writing of the period before 1939, 35–55 per cent of the Jewish population in most countries derived their income from one form or another of business, banking or brokerage, whereas the total percentage of the population in those same countries who engaged in commerce was not higher than 12–15 per cent—even in such essentially mercantile countries as the United States, Great Britain and Germany.

From the point of view of Jewish psychology, should we conclude from these statistics that it was their predilection for business that led the Jews to adopt commercial professions, or that they had perforce to enter them because they were the only professions open to them? A great many Jews have climbed in the short span of two generations from the bottom of the social and economic scale to positions of wealth and importance. The most obvious conclusion to be drawn from their rapid success is that they have a special predilection and special talents for business. But before taking up this question of special talents we should mention two other possible motivating factors: ambition, and love of independence. Both would steer them toward careers offering relative freedom and a chance to be their own master. Our own observations of patients tend to corroborate the influence of these two factors in the choice of a career.

It is the opinion of some authors that some Jews are of exceptionally high intellectual and moral caliber.

They have pointed to the tremendous influence Jews have had on humanity through the medium of the prophets of the Old Testament. In more recent times, and particularly during the past 150 years, they have had an enriching influence on western civilization—an influence out of all proportion to their numbers. They have been prominent in the spheres of philosophy, medicine, sociology, psychology, science, law, the arts, and commerce. Moreover, in their ranks have been found men who in themselves have attained the highest degree of civilization. Does this mean that Jews are on the whole a more gifted, more intelligent and more civilized people than the Gentiles? It is not possible to make such an affirmation. One thing, however, can be stated with certainty. In general, the Jews have attached great importance to intellectual and spiritual values.

VII

Should the special gifts of Jews be classified among their hostility-provoking attributes? There can be no doubt that Jewish achievements in so many fields of human endeavor have increased general hostility toward them, by arousing envy and jealousy and apprehension.

Statistics show that Jews engage more often in business, banking and brokerage than in manual employment. All these preferred professions involve the handling of money. There is no doubt that money has held more varied significance for the Jews than for most other peoples. Most of the Jewish temporal aspirations have centered on money, because of the lack of other outlets. And for several centuries money represented their only means of surviving persecution and expulsion.* Even after their legal emancipation, money remained one of the few means, together with intellectual and artistic achievement, of acquiring a respected and respectable social status. Moreover, for men who have suffered humiliations, money is a tool of revenge and rehabilitation.

It is a mistake to assume that all Jews are inordinately fond of money or that money represents the be-all and end-all of their endeavors. On the contrary, their general attitude toward it has been a mixture of covetousness and contempt. For example, the dream of almost every Jew who has acquired riches is to see his son devote his life to disinterested studies, and in Eastern Europe an orthodox business man prefers to give his daughter in marriage to a poor man dedicated to the study of religion.

Contrary to the generally accepted belief, there are far more poor Jews than rich ones. We must remember that the great majority of Jews in Eastern Europe have lived in a state of appalling poverty and have had no reason whatsoever to vaunt their superior business talents. Non-Jews, however, have always held an exaggerated opinion of the financial talents of the Jews, together with a superstitious belief that all their successes in material and intellectual fields are achieved in mysterious and illicit ways. Add to this the psychological ambivalence aroused in most human beings by money and the possession of money, and it is easy to

* This is again true in our times.

understand how the sweeping generalizations about the Jews and money have arisen. Popular opinion is far more readily built up on rumors and impressions than on objectively observed facts.

VIII

One of the most frequently voiced generalizations about Jews is that they are dishonest in financial transactions. Yet crime statistics do not support this charge. This is clear from statistics on crime among the Jews of Prussia compiled by Ruppin in the period before 1914 and from a similar statistical study on Polish Jews made by Leibman Hersch in the period between the two World Wars. For example, in Warsaw, the crime rate in such categories as theft, receipt and sale of stolen goods, swindling, abuse of office and venality, was more than three times lower among the Jewish than among the non-Jewish population.

These statistics also brought to light many interesting facts on criminality in general among the Jewish and non-Jewish populations. In Poland the general crime rate was twice as low among Jews as among non-Jews. For political offences it was four to five times lower (which would tend to refute the common belief that Jews foster unrest and revolution), and five to six times lower for such crimes as infanticide, homicide, etc.

These statistics are all the more striking in view of the fact that at the time they were made the Jews comprised about 10 per cent of the total population. Moreover, they were compiled on a preponderantly urban population of relatively low economic level, where the crime rate is generally higher.

Furthermore, there were found to be differences in the type of crime most prevalent in the Jewish group. There are fewer crimes of violence and alcoholism, but a greater number of occupational crimes, such as swindling. Ruppin drew the conclusion, which is also valid for the Polish statistics, that the Jew is more prone to transgress the law by intellectual means than by acts of violence.

In the United States also, the crime rate among Jews is lower than that of the general population. Nathan Goldberg, in an article written in 1945,* stated that both in juvenile delinquency and in adult crime, the Jewish percentage was far below the general record in the United States. He gave the following statistics for New York State, where the Jewish population was estimated at 17 per cent of the total population:

ADULTS: 1930 to 1941: Percentage of Jews in New York State prisons varied from 7.2 to 9.6

JUVENILES: Jewish boys in reformatories:
1930: 10.8 per cent of total
1941: 3.3 per cent of total

The American Jewish Congress, in a 1940 survey of the inmates of state penal and correctional institutions, gives the following statistics:**

* *National Jewish Monthly*, Vol. 59, No. 11, July–Aug. 1945.
** These seven states hold about three fourths of American Jewry, estimated at about 4 per cent of the total population.

1939	Jewish percentage of prison inmates	Jewish percentage of state population
Illinois	1.52	5
Massachusetts	2.23	5.4
Michigan	1.42	2
New Jersey	1.9	6
New York (prisons	8.4	17.2
(reformatories	2.2	
Ohio (1938)	1.1	2.79
Pennsylvania	1.2	4.5

Among the factors which make for differences among Jews, one of the most important has been the impact of the various cultures to which they have been exposed. Cultural influences have been strongest in countries where Jews have been treated on terms of equality for a long period of time. In fact, the Jew may sometimes exhibit the national traits of his adopted country in their most exaggerated form. This has given rise to the malicious saying, "Every country has the Jews it deserves."

There are also the differences brought about by the superimposing and intermingling of the many widely divergent cultural patterns they have acquired in the course of their numerous migrations.

The Jewish religion is another cultural element which makes for difference. There is first of all the difference between various sects: orthodox, hassidic, or reformed Judaism. There is an important difference in the degree of religious attachment. There are also two very definite ways in which religion has an influence on practical affairs. One is the fact that worldly success is by no means displeasing in the sight of God. The other is the fact that religious observance is not confined to ceremonies performed at prescribed times in appointed places. Almost every act of daily living is sanctified by God, so that many of the activities which remain purely secular for Christians, such as eating and working, are fraught with religious significance for Jews.

As a consequence, there is little room left in the moral code of the religious Jew for anything corresponding to the Christian secular code of good manners and social etiquette. Once they have fulfilled their prescribed duties toward God—and these, as we know, are numerous—orthodox Jews set little store by such conventions as "what is done" or "what is not done."* This accounts for the impression of Jewish bad manners, which so often shock the non-Jew and which may sometimes have quite far-reaching psychological effects.

One of my patients gave a typical description of the feelings aroused by Jewish manners. Born and brought up in California, she had known no Jews before coming to New York. She is not anti-Semitic. She told me that the first time she walked through a district inhabited almost exclusively by poor Jewish merchants and peddlers, she was so appalled by the thought that these people, who seemed so foreign and totally ignorant of the code of ordinary decent behavior, might one day grow rich and move into her neighborhood.

---

* Geoffrey Gorer has observed that the Japanese attach far greater importance to rigid social conventions than western peoples. There is probably about as wide a gap between the importance given them by western peoples and by strictly orthodox Jews.

She was far less upset when she passed through Italian, Greek or Irish slums, because she felt that there the police would be able to cope with any acts of rowdyism. But what she found so threatening in the Jewish quarter was quite outside the jurisdiction of the police, expressed in their lack of manners. Apart from the underlying personal reasons, this patient's reaction does seem to be quite typical.

It is quite possible that Jewish "bad manners"—or more accurately, Jewish "different manners"—are more often encountered nowadays, since the economic and social mobility of the modern world has greatly increased the number of *nouveau-riche* Jews, many of whom have passed from a state of extreme poverty to one of ease or wealth in the course of a single generation. Their success has been correspondingly rapid and spectacular in the intellectual field.

The ostentatious, patronizing, arrogant behavior of some Jews is another source of irritation to Gentiles, since it contains disguised elements of hostility which are recognized as such by both Jews and Gentiles. These successful Jews are trying to compensate for all the humiliations they suffered in the past not only because they were poor but because they were Jews. It is in some ways an attempt to rehabilitate the whole Jewish people through their own success.

IX

There is one other aspect of the question of Jewish traits on which we have statistical data, and that is the incidence and types of mental and psychic disorder among Jews.

The number of Jewish mental patients in psychiatric wards has been found to be proportionate to their numbers in the population served by the hospital. It is only in the types of psychoses that differences are found. Among Jewish patients there is a relatively low rate of insanity due to so-called organic disturbances—those due to alcoholism or organic brain lesions, for example—whereas there is a high rate of schizophrenic and manic-depressive types. The latter forms of insanity have this in common: first, little is known of their organic causes, and second, although based on hereditary predisposing factors, their onset is often traceable to circumstances or events in the life of the patient which cause psychological trauma. Some psychiatrists believe that the fact that Jews are so frequently exposed to psychologically traumatic experiences accounts for the comparatively high incidence among them of these forms of mental illness.

It is possible, too—although statistics are inadequate on the subject—that there is a higher rate of neuroses among Jews than among non-Jews, and that there are more cases of obsessional neuroses. Also, it would seem that anguish and anxiety are the predominant symptoms in the neuroses of Jews.

Are there any specifically "Jewish" types of neurosis? Actually there are not. All types of mental disturbance are common to the whole western civilization, to Jew and non-Jew alike. But the fact that certain types of neurosis are more prevalent among Jews than among Gentiles has led to their being associated with Jews in the mind of the general public, and in the mind of the patient.

Other neurotic symptoms which occur frequently

among Jews are hypochondriasis, and a propensity—among orthodox Jews—to suffer from disorders of the digestive system. There is also a high incidence of what, since Freud, has been called "character neurosis," in which there occurs a pathological exaggeration of certain characteristics which are common to all humanity but which seem to be found with particular intensity and frequency among Jews.

Let us take some of the typically neurotic traits which are at the root of so much anti-Jewish criticism. First let us consider their attitude toward the possession and use of money. At one end of the scale there are the penny pinchers who, even if they possess wealth, dread its becoming known. Obsessed by the fear of being robbed or envied, they become compulsively secretive and miserly. At the other extreme are the people who make a childish and exaggerated display of their wealth. They are spendthrift to the point of extravagance, driven in their spending by a compulsion to efface their sense of inferiority. It is obvious that both the miserly and the spendthrift type are exaggerations of attitudes toward money common to all human beings. We cannot say with certainty that they are more common among Jews than among, say, Frenchmen or Americans; but it is possible that they are, in view of the fact that money has always had a special social and historical significance for Jews.

There is also the type of neurotic who "always knows better than anyone else," his arrogance a composite of superiority and inferiority feelings; and the victim of chronic anxiety, obsequious when fearful, insolent when protected; or again, there is the confirmed pessimist, prisoner of his fears and forebodings for the future.

Given the following description of an adolescent, one would expect him to be a Jew: "Physically weak, clumsy in games and sports, unpopular with his comrades; but intelligent and ambitious, a hard worker and a good pupil, though perpetually overanxious." Of course by no means all Jewish adolescents answer this description, but it is probably more typical of them than of non-Jewish adolescents, at any rate in the United States.

These character neuroses usually affect the relations of the Jews with the Gentile world and with their fellow Jews in one of two directions: either they suffer from an exaggerated terror of anti-Semitism, or else from a feeling of terror at being Jewish—the latter in its worst form being coupled with anti-Semitism.

These pathological exaggerations are the result of circumstances that can be summed up in one sentence: "It is not easy to be a Jew."

Modern anthropologists* have stressed the fundamental importance on the shaping of a given culture of the child-rearing patterns of the group. It is impossible to make a comparable survey of the child-rearing patterns of the Jews because they are not a homogeneous group and have been exposed to many widely divergent cultural influences. However, from general observations, several significant features in the Jewish methods of raising their children emerge. Jewish parents generally show very strong devotion and attachment to their children. Boys and girls are treated very differ-

* Such as Margaret Mead, Gregory Bateson, and others.

ently, according to the principles of patriarchal societies. Only the boys receive early religious instruction. This fact is extremely important in determining the general attitude of religious Jews toward their children. Circumcision has had an important and dual influence on the boys. The religious Jew, like the Arab, is proud of being circumcised and considers uncircumcised people unclean. But, on the other hand, a Jewish child raised in a Christian community may be made ashamed of his circumcision by the taunts of his companions, and he may acquire a deep and lasting feeling of inferiority as a result.*

Some interesting facts on the maternal attitude of Jewish women are contained in a comparative study made on three groups of fifty families each, selected from among the Jewish, Polish and Negro population of one of the poorer districts in Chicago. The Jewish mother was found to be overanxious, obsessed with the idea that her infant was not getting enough to eat, forcing him by all sorts of means to take nourishment, and weaning him much later than mothers in the two other groups.

Another manifestation of this overanxious behavior is the tendency of Jewish mothers to make their children overfearful in the face of physical danger. This maternal attitude discourages the normal childhood desire to seek parental approval through a show of physical strength and prowess.

It is easy to trace the origins of this overfearful

---

* In the United States the practice of circumcision has been adopted by such a large majority of the Gentile population that it has lost much of its importance as a predisposing factor in Jewish neuroses.

attitude. In Eastern Europe, Jewish children have always run the risk of being beaten up when they passed through the Gentile districts. Because of the very real danger of general reprisals and also because of their characteristic horror of physical violence, their parents generally forbade them to retaliate when they were attacked and taught them instead to take physical refuge in flight and mental refuge in disdain for brute force. Naturally a child reared under such conditions will tend to be fearful and to repress all physical expression of aggression. The comparatively low rate of crimes of violence among Jews is probably a reflection of this childhood upbringing. Also, the Jewish tendency to repress the instincts may well be connected with it. For although sexuality is not treated in such a negative and derogatory fashion in the Jewish religion as it is in the Catholic faith, nevertheless there is a definite strain of puritanism, if not of actual asceticism, in the sexual life of religious and traditionalist Jews.

While the Jewish child is discouraged by his parents from any use of force, use of his intellect meets with warm approval. The acquisition of knowledge has always had a religious and traditional value. It has always been part of the religious duty of every Jewish boy to learn to read and write. The tradition has survived to the present day in the desire of all Jewish parents, regardless of their religious convictions or lack of them, to procure the best possible education for their children. There is no doubt that constant encouragement of the intellectual capacities of a child favors their development.

It is also probable that by fostering the precocious

development of his ego, this parental attitude predisposes the child to neurotic disturbances. At any rate, one thing can be said with certainty: the one definitely psychopathological tendency of Jews is to react with anxiety in many situations. There are two kinds of anxiety reactions: those that are to a certain extent "normal"—that is to say, moderate, temporary and adequately under control—and reactions which are intense and permanent and which unquestionably belong in the framework of mental pathology. Jews tend to react with anxiety, and with deeper and more lasting anxiety than non-Jews, in the most varied psychological situations.*

In Eastern Europe the Jews for a long time passed their whole lives under the perpetual menace of pogroms, and their state of apprehension has been transmitted to their descendants. Even in countries where they enjoy equal civil rights with other citizens, the fear of potential danger never leaves them, through identification with other, persecuted, Jews. And certainly events during the past two decades have proved that their fears were not unrealistic. Actual events have far exceeded the worst forebodings of the most anxious and pessimistic.

* The following joke illustrates the chronic anxiety typical of the Eastern European Jew: Moses meets Isaac in a train near Warsaw. "Why," he said, "I thought you lived in the Caucasus." "I did," replied Isaac, "but I've just left. The government gave orders that all donkeys were to be castrated." "But what's that to you?" asked Moses. "Just try to prove to them that you're not a donkey!" replied Isaac.

Another Jewish joke that plays up their chronic anxiety also reveals one of its underlying psychological sources: Two Jews walking home one night saw two men approaching. "Let's run," they said, "they might attack us. There are two of them and we are alone." Like unwanted children who feel rejected and helpless, Jews are defeatist in the face of their non-Jewish adversaries.

X

There are two other traits related to anxiety and fear which would seem to be fairly common among Jews: obsequiousness, and lack of fighting spirit. The Jewish type of obsequiousness is based on intense fear and on a desire to placate the all-powerful enemy, rather than on true submissiveness and humility. It has an undertone of derisive irony, which is why non-Jews find it particularly objectionable.

Lack of courage and fighting spirit seem to be fairly typical of Jews who have lived for a long time in conditions of legal inequality, and hence in a perpetual state of anxiety and fearfulness. Their lack of fighting spirit can also be explained in terms of their cultural heritage. In the Jewish culture, homicide has always been considered as serious a crime as incest and idolatry. According to the teachings of the rabbis, a Jew should let himself be killed rather than commit murder. The Jews have been a peace-loving people for centuries—all the more averse to war, it is true, because they have so rarely been able to identify wholeheartedly with its various causes, but also because they have learned from bitter experience that it is generally the Jew who pays the piper in the end. Military service used to be particularly repugnant to them, because it forced them into conditions of life in which they were prevented from observing the rites of their religion; also because it exposed them to Jew-baiting from which they would not be able to escape. Nevertheless, these same peace-loving, timid, unsoldierly Jews have always given proof of remarkable courage and heroism in holding on to their religious beliefs.

As we have already observed, Jews show the most cowardice in countries where they feel themselves disliked. Where they have lived on an equal footing with other nationals, and have had from early childhood a sense of being an integrated part of the surrounding group, the picture is entirely different. Like all men, Jews fight well in a cause they can feel their own. The way the young Palestinian Jews have fought against the Arabs is a case in point.*

Some traits of Jews seem to be defects of their exceptional qualities. E. A. Hooton has commented that their intellectual qualities are often accompanied by a kind of arrogance. Others have made the same observation. Their arrogance used to be attributed to their conviction of being God's Chosen People. They can, however, point to many real achievements which would reinforce a feeling of intellectual superiority. But we must not forget that there is a tendency inherent in every religious, ethnic or national community to feel superior toward outside groups, so that it is difficult to judge to what extent Jewish feelings of superiority are more widespread or more obnoxious than similar feelings in non-Jews. Superiority feelings cannot really be explained in terms of achievement because they have no rational basis. They are rooted in the primitive and basic narcissism of man.**

---

* In antiquity Jewish mercenaries were highly valued soldiers when led by Jewish officers. During their war against Rome, for example, they demonstrated outstanding courage and fighting ability.

** Narcissism is the term coined by Freud to designate self-infatuation and kindred reactions.

XI

There are two sets of circumstances which have a profound influence on an individual's narcissim: success and failure. Success satisfies it, giving reassurance, self-confidence, and a feeling of being beloved of the gods—as a child feels secure in his parents' love. Failure, on the other hand, is wounding, and gives a feeling of being unloved or even punished by the gods—like a child rejected by his parents. Success means that your god is strong and that you have found favor in his sight. Failure leads you to doubt his omnipotence, or to fear that he is angry and has forsaken you.

The Jews have very often been in situations which have caused them to doubt the power of their God, or at any rate to doubt His love. They have not often as a people enjoyed temporal power or wealth. Only a prodigious *tour de force* has enabled them to allay their doubts and find a way out of their spiritual dilemma. All their trials and tribulations have been regarded as sent by God as punishment for their sins, but also as special proof of his love, since only through suffering could they be made worthy of a covenant with him.

It would be a mistake to assume, however, that this *tour de force* has always proved fully effective. Most Jews suffer from a profound, ineradicable doubt of their own intrinsic worth.

> Therein lies his tragedy; for his feeling of superiority is forever bound up with a feeling of indelible stigma.
> (Jacob Wassermann).

His self-esteem has none of the serenity of certainty. It is restless, and based on doubt, as if he felt a constant need to justify his claim to superiority—to vindicate himself. In short, it compensates for a profound sense of inferiority.

The skepticism of the Jews is also bound up with their insecurity, and arises out of a fear of being betrayed, due to traditional memories of having in the past paid dearly for trustfulness. In its less pleasant aspects this fear manifests itself in destructive criticism, and in a compelling need to prove themselves "smarter" than the other fellow. The Jews have a genius for finding the "weak spot." On the other hand, their skepticism sometimes takes the form of a fine spirit of constructive criticism and is used to serve the ends of justice.

Certain psychological traits related to those described above have been defined by Erik H. Erikson as Jewish "relativism." By this term he attempts to describe the Jews' seeming inability to give wholehearted allegiance to any one set of ideals or theories. This relativism has found its highest expression in revolutionary scientific discoveries which have upset theories previously accepted as absolute truths. In the average Jew, however, according to Erikson, such relativism takes the form of a somewhat ironic skepticism which keeps him from wholehearted participation in either the enthusiasms or the prejudices of the nation of which he is a citizen. It is by no means directed only against non-Jewish ideals. Jews show similar skepticism towards their own.

Jewish skepticism does not exclude a faith in justice, equality and fraternity, for although belief in the world to come is a part of their creed, the Jew expects redress of wrongs here on earth, in contrast to the

Christian, who finds solace for his earthly sufferings in his faith in a better world to come. Most Jews hold the conviction that through reason and knowledge justice can be achieved and its benefits enjoyed in this earthly life.

This conviction is one of the sources of the charge that all Jews have revolutionary leanings. They are rarely thoroughgoing revolutionaires, however, because although they may be drawn to revolutionary ideas by their strong sense of justice and fraternity, their zeal is often counterbalanced by disillusioned defeatism. The Jew has ceased to believe in justice for himself. But having once placed justice on a pedestal, he keeps it there, without much faith in its ultimate triumph, but without the power to abandon faith.

Whenever they encounter the same ideals and principles among the Gentile host nations, the Jews are ready to emerge from their spiritual isolation and fuse with their fellow citizens, espousing their causes, enthusiasms and feuds. But where they find a great discrepancy between the professed ideal and the reality, they tend to drift into the attitude of critical irony so often held against them.

XII

The Jews' feelings of fear and distrust of Christians are often a facet of their deep-rooted rancor against their persecutors throughout two thousand years of history. Christians, aware of this underlying rancor, often assume it where it does not exist. In this respect both Christians and Jews are like patients suffering from delusions of persecution. They hurl mutual accusations of ill-will, externalizing their own emotions without regard to the reality situation. It would be hard to deny, however, that Jews have incomparably more justification for fearing the ill-will of Gentiles than the Gentiles that of the Jews.

Fear and distrust are not their only reactions to Christians, however. Many Jews have a profound admiration for Christianity and Christian ethics. Some adopt Christianity and others only refrain from doing so through the moral scruple of being considered renegades. Jewish patients in analysis often have fantasies in which they identify with Christ and dream of sharing his fate. And how often Jews feel that they are better Christians than the Christians. Recently such Jewish writers as Sholem Asch and Klausner have stressed the intimate bonds between Pharisaical Judaism and primitive Christianity. In doing so they have taken a great step toward eliminating one of the most tragic conflicts that confront the Jews—that of living in a civilization so deeply permeated with the Christian religion, of which their ancestors were part generators, and yet from which they feel themselves excluded.

XIII

The attitude of the Jews toward the Christian world can only be understood in conjunction with their attitude toward themselves, which it might be well to recapitulate here.

The Jews' all-pervading anxiety and psychic malaise together form what is commonly known as an "inferiority complex." This amalgam of reactions generally consists of feelings of insecurity accompanied by feelings of guilt and self-consciousness. Such feelings derive in the first place from the unique social status of the Jews, which is without precedent or parallel in the history of mankind. They are a "people," an ethnic group, without a homeland, living in dispersion among other peoples. Until quite recent times a part of them, in Eastern Europe, lived in complete spiritual and cultural isolation from the surrounding populations. In other parts of the world they have had much closer contact with the host nations and attained a considerable degree of assimilation; in Western Europe and in the United States, they have acquired the national characteristics, language and customs of their hosts and have adopted their causes and prejudices and shared their victories and defeats. They have, in fact, become integrated into their adopted nations. Nevertheless they continue to have moments of acute awareness of the almost imperceptible ties which bind them to all the other members of the dispersed group, with whom their only point in common is that they are Jews.

They are thus in a state of perpetual apprehension, and feel a constant need for reassurance. They are always on the defensive, crying down their critics and proving their innocence even when they have not been accused of anything. Some who have lived in an atmosphere of recriminations and persecutions all their lives come to lay the blame for all their failures and frustrations at the door of anti-Semitism, closing their eyes to any personal shortcomings or inadequacies that could be partially responsible. On the other hand, a Jew may attribute his failure or ostracism to his personal inadequacy when actually it has been determined by his being a Jew.

Sometimes, under the pressure of agonizing and humiliating racial memories, Jews develop such an insurmountable terror of anti-Semitism that they are prone to feel themselves insulted and attacked whenever a Gentile so much as pronounces the word "Jew," and the mildest anti-Jewish remark may throw them off balance, plunging them into outraged silence or excessive rage. Only rarely are they able to meet such remarks calmly, or to parry them with a humorous reply.

XIV

In their struggle for survival the Jews have often been forced to ask hospitality of those countries where they could hope for some measure of protection against persecution. As a consequence they have developed a feeling of obligation toward their hosts, and when a feeling of obligation exists, as it does wherever they are not living in complete spiritual isolation, it implies an inclination toward assimilation. This in turn results in a special type of reaction toward the rest of the Jewish world, with which they are thenceforward only partially identified.

This brings us back to the conflicting attitudes of Jews toward their fellow Jews; in other words, to the question of Jewish anti-Semitism—outcome of the continual social and psychological pressures of their situation as a permanent minority group. The inevitable consequence of this situation has been what Anna Freud has called "identification with the aggressor," the aggressor in this case being the Gentile anti-Semite.

Some types of Jewish anti-Semitism can be explained in terms of defensive reactions against "faults" for which they feel no personal responsibility. A Jew may suffer in the presence of a less well-assimilated Jew and may find in him such "Jewish traits" as tactlessness or arrogance. He may be ashamed of this other Jew and resent him as a poor relation is resented who brings ridicule on the family. It is of no avail that he feels completely different; there yet remains some sort of secret tie between him and this other Jew, a bond of mutual responsibility. Such a reaction is of course common to all minority groups, but it is accentuated in the Jewish minority because Jews know that inevitably non-Jews will attribute the objectionable traits of an individual Jew to all Jews. Hence their hypersensitivity to the shortcomings of members of their own family. On the other hand, they sometimes adopt the reverse attitude and display an insensitivity to other peoples' feelings which their non-Jewish neighbors find hard to forgive.

The special element in all such reactions is their anti-Semitic nature. Jews find in one another the identical faults that anti-Semites find in them. One Jew will say of another, "Now there's a dirty Jew if ever there was one!" The difference between him and a genuine anti-Semite is that he dislikes a specific Jew, while still considering Jews in general admirable people. The anti-Semites are firmly convinced that "the Jews" should be wiped off the face of the earth, yet they may have close personal Jewish friends whom they respect and admire.

There are a few cases—particularly among neurotics and recent converts—in which Jewish anti-Semitism reaches Nazi proportions, but the great majority of Jews are not even conscious of harboring anti-Semitic feelings, which only emerge under special conditions, such as pressure of conflicting loyalties.

During the past few decades the "inferiority complex" is appreciably on the wane in one important Jewish group, the Zionists.* They are intensely aware of the implications of the "abnormal" social and economic status of world Jewry, and pin their hopes for the future on a normalization of their status. Even among Zionists, however, inferiority feelings have not been entirely eradicated. Sometimes they have become reversed and are manifested in extreme chauvinism. Their chauvinism is another form of "identification with the aggressor," in which the Jews follow the common trend of minorities in modern times, reacting to the hostility of the majority which rejects them in the name of nationalism by adopting a nationalism of their own.

XV

In summing up, it may be said that all so-called Jewish psychological traits are common to all human beings. However, sometimes they may take on a special tinge due to the special situation in which Jews live. And here we are not referring to the pitiful survivors of concentration camps. We are referring to the Jews who live in comparative peace and security. Even for them, their Jew consciousness is easily convertible into a factor of trouble. The fact of being American or English or French is natural and taken for granted by Americans, Englishmen or Frenchmen. But the fact of

---

* I can only refer to the Zionists of Europe and America, since I have had no opportunity to observe Palestinian Jews.

being Jewish is not so simple for the Jew. Almost invariably it invokes in him a defensive attitude, in response to an inner perturbation compounded of all the outrages ever perpetrated against the Jewish people in time and space.

Small wonder then that the fact of being Jews sometimes weighs upon them so heavily that their one desire is to rid themselves of the stigma. The more neurotic may deny their Jewish origins in the face of most palpable evidence to the contrary. Others may become pathologically anti-Semitic. Generally, however, the pendulum swings to the other extreme and they cling tenaciously to their Jewishness.

The capacity to carry Jewishness well depends on the absence of factors predisposing to neurosis. There is no getting away from the fact, however, that even for the most well-adjusted, it is not easy to be a Jew. Many have been psychologically damaged by feelings that they are not like other people. Others again have benefited by their "exceptional" status, and through it have developed a breadth of vision and depth of human understanding that have made them in truth exceptional. But even these outstanding Jews are not proof against anguish and self-torture, nor immune to the ambivalent reactions of the Gentile world.

II. The Marginal Man

I

According to Toynbee, the Jews are fossils of the ancient Syriac society, who survived into the Greco-Roman civilization. A small remnant of Yemenite Jews, such as the Falachas in Abyssinia and the Caucasian

Jews, managed to survive in a kind of "fastness." The Falachas maintained themselves as a politically independent nation in the high plains of Abyssinia until the beginning of the nineteenth century, when they were conquered by the Abyssinians. These isolated, independent Jewish communities had to struggle with nature for their subsistence, but for the great majority of Jewish groups living scattered among the Gentiles as "penalized minorities," the struggle has not been against nature but against a hostile social environment. To quote Toynbee:

> If they survive at all they succeed in holding their own by learning to excel in the narrow field of social activity to which their Gentile neighbors and masters are apt to confine them. The tyrannical and malignant exclusion from certain walks of life is apt to stimulate them in fields which still have been left open to them. But a penalization which truly stimulated the penalized minority to a heroic response is as truly apt to warp their human nature; as a consequence all these penalized minorities (Levantines, Phanariots, Armenians, Jews) have the reputation of being "not as other men are" for worse or for better.

Toynbee's theory does not, however, explain all aspects of the problem. It does not take sufficiently into account the active participation of the Jews in the shaping of the modern world and their major contributions to civilization, which have been no negligible factors in the formation of the so-called Jewish traits and in the Gentile reactions to them.

Recently the theory of the "marginal man" has been evolved by sociologists to describe human groups which, for racial, social or cultural reasons, are outside the dominant social group. Here is Stonequist's definition:

> The marginal man is the individual who lives in, or has ties of kinship with, two or more interacting societies between which there exists sufficient incompatibility to render his own adjustment to them difficult or impossible. He does not quite "belong" or feel at home in either group. This feeling of homelessness or of estrangement does not arise in the same way or for the same reasons in all individuals, nor is it identical in all situations. For many it is a matter of incomplete cultural assimilation in one or both societies, for others it arises less because of lack of cultural assimilation than from failure to gain social acceptance, and in some cases it originates less because of obvious external barriers than because of persistent inhibitions and loyalties.
>
> In some situations the determining factor in the creation of the marginal personality is the degree of cultural difference between the groups in contact. In other situations the basic factor is biological or racial. And there are other situations where both the cultural and racial differences are nonexistent or of minor importance but where the estrangement continues because of the carry-over of traditional attitudes from the past and from other areas. This is particularly true of the modern Jew in certain communities.
>
> The exact nature of marginality, its intensity, psychological qualities, the social role it educes, its pattern of changes and solution—these differ in accordance with the nature of the situation.

From Stonequist's description it would seem that the characteristics which we described earlier as "Jewish" traits are typical of all "marginal" groups.

A "marginal" situation produces excessive feelings of inferiority and as a result of these, aggressive behavior toward the dominant group. This in turn increases the reverse antagonism of the dominant group. Sometimes, as a result of his ambiguous situation, the marginal man becomes an insidious and merciless critic of the dominant group. He combines the intuitive perception of the insider with the critical objectivity of the outsider. He becomes very skillful in unmasking hypocrisies and in finding the cracks in the armor, and as a consequence falls easily into the attitude, if not the active role, of radical or revolutionary.

The marginal man can meet his problem either by merging completely with the dominant group or by identifying with the subordinate group. If he chooses the first course the problem of marginality will generally resolve of itself in the course of time. The second course may lead to a repression of the conflict, or to its sublimation in the role of some sort of intermediary, or to the adoption of a narrow nationalism of his own. It quite often happens that the two attitudes coexist in the same individual. The resultant stress and strain of divided allegiance create the ambivalent attitudes and emotions so characteristic of the marginal individual. He is perpetually torn between hatred and resentment of the dominant group and hatred and resentment of his own group.

The conflict may flare up suddenly, as when a child, or an adult, abruptly realizes that the color of his skin or the fact of belonging to a mysterious clan called "Jews" makes him different from and inferior to his fellows. This may bring on an acute crisis which will have to be dealt with in one of the above ways.

Sometimes the marginal status of a man is the end result of a chain of circumstances set in motion by the initial fact of being a foreigner. When two nations or two cultures clash the role of intermediary has generally developed upon those who have had a "foot in both camps." Consequently the Jews have held this intermediary role many times in their history. When they have used their familiarity with two cultures in a creative way genuinely "internationally minded" men have devolved—rare individuals who are in no way to be confused with uprooted cosmopolitans who have no real ties with any culture or tradition.

Solution of the conflict through assimilation may sometimes take the form of camouflage, whereby a member of a subordinate group seeks to "pass" into the dominant one. This is the case when a Jew is baptized a Christian for reasons of expediency or social ambition rather than because of religious conviction.

The cultural conflicts involved in the marginal status are held responsible for serious psychological damage. The impressively high suicide rate among immigrants is cited as proof. The rate is considerably higher than that of the native-born population and higher than that of the same nationals in their homeland. However, there is an even higher suicide and delinquency rate among the native-born children of immigrants than among their foreign-born parents; that is, among partially assimilated individuals in conflict with nonassimilated parents. This bears out the repeated observations of psychoanalysis—that the most damaging of all psychological conflicts are those which occur between parents and children. In the case of the children of immigrants the damage is all the more severe because the parental conflict is reinforced by a cultural conflict.

There can be no doubt that a marginal status accounts for some of the Jewish traits, but it by no means explains the whole problem nor even the whole sociological problem. It does not explain, for example, why the Jews, who are subject to the same conditions which lead to an increase in criminality in other marginal groups, have a considerably lower crime rate than the non-Jewish populations. Neither does it explain the differences in types of criminality.

In every human being one can find reflections of all the individuals with whom he can identify—with individuals of the same country, of the same race, of the same religion. There are several of these "systems" in every man, in terms of which identifications may conflict.* Individuals belonging to a subordinate group may identify with the dominant group and its ideals. Hence a marginal man sometimes feels some of the contempt and hostility toward the subordinate group that the dominant group shows. Identification with the dominant group explains why among North American Negroes there may be contempt for the darker-skinned, the implicit ideal being to look as much like the white race as possible. The adaptation mechanism of "identification with the aggressor" is by no means confined to marginal peoples, but is a phenomenon known to occur under given conditions. German political internees, after they had lived through two or three years of imprisonment and torture, sometimes ended up by imitating as closely as possible the conduct and mannerisms and even the clothes of their SS torturers.

There are some other sociological aspects of the problem. All human beings seem to be bound to the

* Needless to say, the personality is not exclusively made up of these various identifications.

communities of which they are a part by some sort of tacit contract of mutual rights and duties. This contract forms an unconscious moral bond on which the moral code of the individuals composing the community is based. It is built up on feelings of mutual confidence and acceptance, and on an expectancy of just dealings between individuals within the community. This tacit contract manifests itself in a thousand ways in daily living: in idioms of speech, fashions in dress, eating habits, social etiquette. Every individual born or accepted into the community expects as a matter of course to receive the same treatment as every other member. In the case of the Jews, this tacit contract has been broken so frequently at their expense that some of them have come to feel justified in not living up to it, in anticipation of possible infringement on the part of the community. Such behavior is typical of people of "exceptional" status, who tend to be full of recriminations, to nurse grudges, and to brood over past grievances.

III. Psychoanalysis of the Jews

I

The sociological approach to our problem, however illuminating, is nevertheless not completely satisfactory because it gives only a "cross-sectional" picture of individuals and groups. The psychoanalytic method tackles the problem from the angle of development. It attempts to describe the forces at work from the point of view of the history of the individual in a changing environment. Obviously the method will have to be revised and adapted if it is to be applied with equal validity to the study of the evolution of a group in a changing historical environment.

Freud used psychoanalysis for an interpretative history of the human race, using a procedure similar to that employed in the analysis of an individual. The nation, or the race, was considered as a single individual whose distant past—its forgotten prehistory, as it were—could be reconstructed from the traces left in its representative works, in its traditions and in its destiny. This method is open to criticism for two reasons. First, because it is based on the improbable hypothesis of a parallel between the development of individuals and the development of humanity in general. Secondly, because it presupposes the hereditary transmission of racial memories. The latter hypothesis presents such tremendous difficulties that we prefer to proceed without it. And we may safely do so because there is another way in which psychoanalysis can be used as a tool for the study of a group instead of an individual.

In the psychoanalysis of an individual, his life history is studied within the framework of his changing, but known, social milieu. We know that the life history of every human being is influenced from his early infancy by the behavior of his parents and by the cultural and social environment, and that these influences in turn reflect the history of the group into which the child is born. Thus the analytic method can be expanded into a study of a group by evaluating the psychic processes of an individual in a given generation in so far as he mirrors the influence of the group history, and by considering the extent to which the life pattern of this individual influences in turn his social environment and hence modifies in some degree the patterns which will be handed down to succeeding generations.

In describing the psychological traits of Jews, our procedure has been to establish which situations are common to a great number of them, and more therefore than the chance product of individual circumstances. The personality of the individual Jew is evolved not only from a complex of factors common to all human beings but also from certain factors specifically connected with his being a Jew, or a member of a particular Jewish community or family. He is exposed to the reciprocal influence of individual, family, social and historical factors. His childhood will be influenced by the personality, behavior and social situation of his parents. Chiefly through identification with his parents and also, as far as the formation of his superego is concerned, by his taking over of the parental superego. Later his life pattern may be further influenced by such events as being ostracized by non-Jewish children; later still, by the choice of professions open, or closed, to him and by his marginal status, and so forth. The gruelling social pressures to which the Jew is exposed are well known. On one hand, the non-Jewish environment subjects him to varying degrees of anti-Semitism—from almost imperceptible irony to open and violent hostility—and on the other hand, in the family environment, he feels the whole impact of Jewish traditions, heavy with ancestral memories of past persecutions and with forebodings of persecutions to come.

II

Let us consider the reactions of the type of individuals—Jews and non-Jews alike—whom Freud has called "exceptions," because they see themselves as such. He quotes cases of neurotic patients who unconsciously, and sometimes even consciously, consider themselves unjustly treated by fate and who consequently claim special treatment and special privileges in life. Freud cites as the archetype of this personality Shakespeare's Richard III, who was born deformed and claimed the right to avenge this affront of destiny by acts of cruelty against more fortunate and better-favored mortals.

Naturally most of the people who consider themselves exceptions do not go to such extremes as Richard III. But they all have a tendency to claim special rights and exemptions to compensate for what they consider injustices. Feeling themselves different from other men, they adopt an attitude of superiority (and at the same time of inferiority) toward the ordinary run of mortals. Sometimes an infirmity may become a source of special pride and vanity, but it is never a calm untroubled pride. It is always based on fear, nonacceptance and need for compensation.

Jews find themselves in "exceptional" situations far more frequently than do non-Jews. Indeed, we have seen that their whole pattern of evolution has been to a great extent determined by the fact that, since the dispersion, they have been a unique social phenomenon in western civilization, and that they have had an exceptional status in the Christian religion. The exceptional status conferred on them by the non-

Jewish world has been reinforced by their own race consciousness. They have from the beginning of their history believed themselves to be God's Chosen People with the predestined role of Priest People for the whole world in the Messianic Age to come. They have also felt themselves to be exceptional in the amount of suffering they have been called upon to bear, and because in spite of it they have managed to survive and to preserve their identity as a group.

We have already mentioned how often Jews feel that the tacit social contract is broken at their expense and how they sometimes assume the right to infringe it themselves on account of long-past grievances. There is an obvious analogy between the Jewish "exceptional" psychology and the psychology of children who are exposed to continual censure from sadistic or neurotic parents or teachers. The child's guilt feelings are intensified, he becomes hypersensitive to criticism, he feels a constant need for self-justification and yet is peculiarly inept and uneasy in exonerating himself; he is forever appealing to justice and yet suspicious of all moral standards since they appear to him to serve only as pretexts for injustices and wrong dealing. In short, such a child displays many of the traits frequently observed in the Jewish personality.

III

The mechanism underlying the special reactions of Jews wrongfully accused was made clear to me one day by the late Dr. Hanns Sachs. He was referring to the paradoxical behavior of innocent people who appear overcome with guilt when accused of misdeeds they have not committed. The reason for their inhibited and uneasy behavior in clearing themselves is because behind their affirmations of innocence lies the consciousness of other inadmissible and blameworthy acts or intentions. Freud first observed that as much guilt is felt for unrealized intentions as for deeds actually committed. The Catholic Church has recognized this in defining the "sin of intention."

To take only one example: The French Jews hoped that victory over Germany would bring an end to Nazi anti-Semitism—a hope shared by many other Frenchmen. After the defeat of France, the Vichy Government seized upon this known fact to accuse the Jews of having engineered the war and led France to her ruin. Obviously there was a vast difference between the unvoiced wishes of the majority and the political acts of a few Jews, and the actual outbreak of the war and its subsequent disastrous conclusion. Nevertheless after the armistice of 1940, the Jews found themselves in a psychologically awkward position in the face of the Vichy Government's accusations. It was the juxtaposition of the two "crimes"—the real "crime" of having desired the defeat of Nazi Germany, and the unjustly imputed "crime" of having engineered the war and the subsequent defeat. It gave the Jews an uneasy feeling of guilt against which it was hard to defend themselves; all the harder, it is true, because the Vichy Government made it materially impossible for them to prove their innocence.

Freud also described a certain type of delinquent whose crimes derive from feelings of guilt. Such a delinquent commits a crime because he is unconsciously seeking punishment for guilt-laden unconscious desires. This situation is more apt to arise when the guilt feelings are of a "borrowed" nature; that is to say, when the subject feels guilty of sins that are not his own but which he has taken over or "borrowed" from some one else. Children habitually take over the faults of their parents or others in authority. They are faults which the child has been powerless to accuse them of openly, or against which he has been defenseless. He behaves as if he himself had committed the faults and, curiously, "respects" them, either by behaving like a guilty person himself or by committing other reprehensible acts to rid himself of responsibilities which are not his. There is a striking resemblance between this mechanism and the reactions of some Jews in the face of unjust treatment at the hands of anti-Semites.

Perpetual accusations and breaches of contract finally impinge upon their personality. They become full of self-doubt and self-depreciation. Adults resemble children in that they continue to expect proofs of love from the world, from destiny and from God. The Jews, in spite of their conviction that they are God's favorite sons, experience the miseries they endure as a lack of affection, and like children, they suffer more from a lack of affection than from actual injustices.

We have alluded at several points to the parallel between the reactions of Jews and the reactions of young children. This is more than a mere comparison. In the normal course of existence all children, Jews and Gentiles alike, undergo a certain amount of unjust treatment at the hands of their parents. But Jewish children are further humiliated by injustices inflicted on their whole family by the outside world, and this may become a factor of increased resentment against the parents for being powerless to protect them from it. It more often happens, however, that family ties are strengthened thereby, and the whole complex of hostility is directed against the extrafamilial hostile world. When an adult Jew first experiences injustice because he is a Jew, it rekindles infantile states of mind that were never entirely eradicated and stimulates infantile reactions in response not only to the adult situation but also to the traditional memories of injustices instilled in him in childhood.

IV

What is the genesis of the "exceptional" status of the Jews which has been such a psychological troublemaker throughout their history? It is certain that the most serious traumatic experience in the history of the Jewish people was the destruction of the second Temple and of Jerusalem in 70 A.D. Their exceptional status dates from that event. When they lost Palestine, they lost both their national home and the religious center around which were focused all the rites and ceremonies and the innumerable traditional procedures of the Hebrew religion. It would seem that they never became reconciled to their loss. The ritual phrase "next year in Jerusalem" may be without meaning or reality for some Jews, yet for others it has retained its full emotional and intellectual significance.

According to Freud, mourning after the death of a love object is made up of a great many psychological processes which together form the mourning process. The mourning process operates under the sign of two tendencies which are in opposition: the tendency to preserve the memory of the love object and to remain faithful to the dead and detached from outward reality, and the tendency to absorb the shock and liquidate the loss and, with renewed interest in the world of the living, to seek out a fresh love object. The period of mourning is of varying duration, but only exceptionally does it crystallize into permanence. The loss of Jerusalem and of Palestine for the Jewish people can be compared to the loss of a beloved parent or a secure and happy home for an individual. The result for the Jews has been a permanent state of mourning. They have not, however, given equal importance to the three aspects of the lost love—Jerusalem, the native land, political independence—but have concentrated all their regret and nostalgia, all their love and loyalty upon the loss of Jerusalem, the Holy City, Zion. Until recent times grief for the loss of the homeland and of national independence has played a minor role, partly perhaps because of the material impossibility of recovering either—homeland or independence—before the present century.

V

One of the reasons that enabled the Jews to survive the loss of Jerusalem was their propensity to scorn physical violence and temporal power and to prize spiritual values. This tendency was evident long before the second destruction of Jerusalem. For several centuries prior to that event, the great Asiatic kingdoms had dashed all Jewish hopes of an earthly kingdom and all designs for political independence. The only channel that remained for their ambitions was their religion. As Renan observed, it was almost inevitable that such a people would work toward the establishment of a universal, rather than a national or political, institution. This "anomaly" had been an integral part of the evolution of the Jewish people from the time of the destruction of the first Temple and the Babylonian captivity in the sixth century B.C. In fact, it might be said that the Jews were able to survive the loss of the second Temple because their history had prepared them for it. Their religion is what held them together throughout the centuries. And Judaism is the religion of a people whose relations with their God have always taken precedence over their relations with nature or with the state. After the Babylonian exile, the Jews dissociated their God from his earthly habitat in the first Temple, and although later they regained a national homeland, their essential relationship with their God remained independent of political or territorial conditions. After the destruction of the second Temple, the last link between their God and their native land was broken, and thereafter the last traces of "tribal provincialism" disappeared.

Among monotheistic peoples, expression of aggression against their God is made impossible, since he is infallible and can do no wrong. When misfortune strikes God cannot be blamed, they must blame themselves. This internalization is a fundamental psychological process, and the basis of the whole mental set of the Jewish people in the face of disaster. Jews have even derived a special satisfaction from their suffering: Jehovah is punishing them for their disobedience and lack of piety; through their suffering they will be restored to His favor. Misfortune, therefore, becomes an indirect proof of Divine Love.

We have no clue to the origin of this unique attitude which was to have such an important influence on the subsequent history of western civilization.* All that we know is that it is based on the concept of God the Father Universal and Unique, and on renunciation of the concept of a maternal deity, which had hitherto been an indispensable element in the pantheons of the primitive populations of Syria and Palesstine.

Other peoples, when defeated by a stronger nation, adopted the gods of their conquerors, whose victory had demonstrated their superiority over their own defeated gods. But Jehovah was a jealous god and would tolerate no other gods. His intolerance was inseparable from His universality, so that Israel, first to conceive of the whole universe as the expression of the will of the one true God, cannot in the face of defeat challenge God's omnipotence or his uniqueness and must not harbor the thought that He has betrayed her. It is from this conception of a universal god that the Jews have drawn their strength and it is to this conception that they owe their survival. Their prophets taught them to despise armed might and to look upon military or political disasters as minor incidents in the unfolding of the all-absorbing central drama of God's relations with the Jewish people. The vast and powerful empires that surrounded the puny little people of Israel were seen as mere puppets in the hands of God,

---

* Freud in his book on *Moses and Monotheism* (Knopf, New York, 1939) formulated the hypothesis that Moses was an Egyptian who transmitted the monotheism of Amenhotep IV or Ikhnaton to the Jews.

used by Him to chastise His favorite children when they deserved punishment.

VI

Psychoanalysis has made possible the study of similar mechanisms in neurotics, particularly in compulsive neurotics. The compulsive neurotic forbids himself any show of aggression against anyone in his immediate environment. Usually when the patient is a man the inhibited aggression was originally experienced against his father, whom he both loved and hated at certain times during childhood. When love prevails the boy will repress all manifestations of aggression against his father and will tend to transform his hostile feelings into feelings of guilt and a need for self-punishment. The compulsive gestures of an obsessional neurotic often have the significance of magic, invoked to avert the possible consequences of his own aggressions. They are in the nature of preventive action or of self-punishment for having harbored hostile intentions toward the object of love and respect.

And as the obsessional neurotic reverses against himself the unconscious aggression originally directed against his father, so the Jewish people turn against themselves the hostility they originally experienced toward God and toward their conquerors.

We have just described how the Jews resolved one of the great moral conflicts which assailed them in times of national disaster. There was also another problem to be faced. They had to choose whether to live a life of scrupulous and rigid observance of the minutiae of ritual procedures, or to give first place to the ethical value of human actions. These interpenetrating problems are the basis of the inner conflicts which have always existed within the Jewish people: and which they have never entirely resolved: the conflict between material and spiritual values, between national and universal aspirations, between violence and nonviolence. During the centuries which preceded the schism between Judaism and Christianity, Pharisaic principles, and a spiritual and universal solution to their problems, gradually gained the ascendancy. Nevertheless, there were still attempts to employ the alternative solution: the revolt of the Maccabeans against forcible Hellenization was one such attempt, and later the disastrous attempt to recover national independence from Rome.

The Jewish people have always been inwardly aware of the possibility of these alternative solutions to their temporal problems, but the solution by nonviolence came to be adopted, and the hope for the establishment of the Kingdom of God by nonviolence and by strict obedience to the Law prevailed. They gradually lost their foothold in material reality, and the Jewish religion was thereby deprived of its national and political foundations.

Nevertheless, it was the budding Christian religion which first developed to extremes the Jewish solution of renunciation of material in favor of spiritual values. The prodigious success of Christianity, once it had been adopted as the state religion by the Roman Empire, gradually dislodged Judaism from its position of universal religion and relegated it to the position of a "closed" religion. The mother religion relinquished the field to her daughter and withdrew into contemplation of the past, without, however, abandoning all hope for the future.

After the final, definitive loss of Palestine, the Jews disappeared as a political entity and acquired a special type of universality, through their self-imposed choice of remaining a landless, countryless people. By the Moslem and Christian peoples among whom they later dwelled, the Jews were regarded as the "People of the Book," both venerated and despised—a sacred people of the same blood as Christ but accursed for having crucified him. In short, thenceforward they were destined to live the abnormal and tragic life of a "tabooed people."

VII

The riddle of the survival of the Jewish people and the Jewish religion is twofold: why did they survive, and how did they survive. In other words, to what psychological and social adaptations do they owe their survival, and how have they paid for this survival?

We have seen how, just when Judaism was on the point of finding a solution to the conflict between ethnico-national ambitions and universal aspirations, Christianity usurped the role of universal religion. The victory of Christianity was facilitated because of the loss of prestige which the Jewish people suffered when their Temple was destroyed. God himself seemed to be refuting their claim of being His Chosen People. Jehovah, once again, lost his only material representation on earth and became even more than formerly an interiorized God, kept alive in the hearts of his devout followers.

During the following centuries the spiritual leaders of Judaism continued the work of codifying the Talmud, and of adapting the ancient laws to the changing conditions of life of the Jews. Their essential aim was to effect this adaptation while remaining faithful at all costs to a past that had no continuity in the present—to the former life of the Jewish people in the land of Palestine, the Promised Land. These opposing tendencies—adaptation to real life and nostalgic clinging to the past—are constantly and conjunctively in evidence in the Jewish religion, and have influenced the Jewish people in one or the other direction throughout their history.*

Judaism's defeat in its struggle with the young Christian religion served to reinforce the sense of mourning and regret for the past. Henceforth the only bonds with temporal reality were material possessions. And the many restrictions with which the Christian world encompassed them confined even these within ever-narrowing limits. Until quite recent times the Jews' search for temporal power never took the form of seeking a new homeland. Judaism remained faithful to Zion. The desire for a homeland was only reactivated when a return to the Palestine they had left twenty centuries before became possible.**

Introversion and nostalgia for the past were intensified during the persecutions of the Middle Ages.

* The most significant example of this conflict is to be found in the two schools that influenced the writing of the Talmud: the narrow rigorism of Shammai and the liberalism of Hillel the Great, ancestor and teacher of most of the great codifiers.
** Their return to Palestine was made materially possible by the victorious powers after the First World War. It was made psychologically possible by the influence on the younger generations of Jews of the strong wave of nationalism which swept through the minorities of Europe.

In this epoch the Jews suffered their second serious trauma, or more correctly, their second series of traumatic experiences, since these extended over several centuries.

A significant foreshadowing of Jewish reactions to a hostile environment is offered by events in Western Europe. Up to the end of the thirteenth century, the rationalist and universalist type of Judaism of Maimonides—fruit of several centuries of tolerance—had prevailed there. But the growing persecutions led to a reverse trend in Judaism. The spiritual leaders of these Jews who were the only literate people in the Middle Ages besides the monks, and through whom the civilizing influences of Greco-Roman and Arabian culture had been transmitted to Europe, now proscribed all profane studies except medicine to Jews under twenty-five. This proscription has been largely responsible for the abhorrence of all learning other than the study of the Torah and the Talmud, which has been characteristic of the strictly orthodox Jews in Eastern Europe.

Throughout the many centuries of the Diaspora, Israel remained faithful to Jerusalem and faithful also to the psychological mechanism whereby the stronger the persecution they endured, the more persistently they looked to their past. From the fourteenth to the eighteenth century, the Jewish people carried this "internalization" to such extremes that for many it had pathological consequences. Psychological isolation is a good breeding ground for neurosis and neurotic personality traits.

Small wonder then that this impassioned devotion to the past has developed somber personalities; for it has been accompanied by dislike and avoidance of reality and by an obsessive overevaluation of the least detail connected with ritualistic procedures and taboos. All the intellectual and emotional energy of devout Jews has been concentrated on an attempt to reconcile the irreconcilable. The ever-changing, ever-painful demands of real life have had to be reconciled with the spirit—and even more with the letter—of traditional laws evolved under totally different life conditions.

Sheltered within the ghetto walls, isolated from the hostile world outside, the Jewish communities devoted their lives to the strict observance of their religion and to the contemplation of their glorious past. The twofold implication of the ghetto walls is symbolically significant of their whole psychological situation in relation to the peoples among whom they have lived. Jewish isolation has always been a sign of both rejection and protection.

If the trauma of the loss of Palestine had not in itself been enough to create the characteristics which have come to be known as typically Jewish, the accumulation of traumatic experiences during the centuries of persecution and of ghetto living did even more serious psychological damage.

VIII

We have seen how during the Diaspora the Jewish people had to learn to confine their worldly ambitions to the narrow sphere of material possessions and money, which is but a pale image, a mere fraction, of the temporal interests of the average people. After their final defeat at the hands of Rome, they renounced temporal ambitions, and chose the way of gentleness instead of the way of force. They never thereafter tried to regain their lost homeland or to conquer a new one. Consequently, the aggressive forces of their men folk were never called into play for the breaking of new ground or the conquering of new lands. Having no land, the Jews have had no "working class." There have of course been Jewish workmen and craftsmen, but there has never been a class tradition of farmers, miners, huntsmen, fishermen, soldiers, sailors, nor of any other of the occupations which call for the exercise of man's aggressive forces. And yet these are the most basic and normal channels in which human aggressions can be employed.

It is true that in every civilized society there are whole classes of people who no longer need to employ their physical force to gain a livelihood. But they are still able to identify with other members of their community who do so earn their living, or they can identify with their national heroes and pioneers through the traditional folklore of the community. But the Jews, inasmuch as they formed Israel in the Diaspora, lacked even this indirect outlet for their aggressions. For the military victories of David and of the Maccabeans have played but a small role in Jewish folklore.

The aggressive drives have much to do with the vital impulses of self-preservation. Man is a part of the animal kingdom and in order to live must destroy living matter, either vegetable or animal. Only organisms which belong to the vegetable kingdom live and obtain nourishment without destroying other living organisms.

We know that the great revolution in the prehistory of the human race was the transformation of the communities of hunters and gatherers of food into communities of farmers and cattle raisers. Immediate destruction of animal or vegetable organisms needed for food was deferred in favor of domestication and cultivation. Men learned to control their destructive instincts temporarily in order to enjoy future gratifications. In spite of the fundamental changes this produced in the economy of the aggressive drives, it did not entirely abolish the intimate relationship between expenditure of physical force in muscular effort and the procuring of food.

The importance of normal labor for emotional balance transcends the framework of the problem of normal utilization of the aggressions in the economy of the mind. It is probable that there are even more complex connections between emotional equilibrium and work, and especially between such equilibrium and the objects created by a man's own hands. Agricultural labor in particular has countless emotional values for man. In addition to the civilizing influence of the formation of agrarian communities, there is also the strong emotional tie between farmers and the natural elements. In some primitive societies these have found expression in symbolic sexual communion with Mother Earth. There is a whole complex of factors here which have obviously had a tremendous influence on the development of the human mind.

Earlier in this chapter we made a distinction between the groups of Jews who have survived in remote regions in isolated communities and those—by far the greater number—who have lived in larger communities as "penalized minorities." The latter because of this peculiar status, have never had to contend with the forces of nature. The dangers they have faced have been man-created, stemming from the forces of human aggression.

When the Jews shut off the normal channels of aggression, they had to find some other means of dealing with their aggressive drives. This they did by means of what Anna Freud has called an "avoidance" mechanism. In a child this consists of the systematic avoidance of those external situations which would place him in a real or imagined inferior light in relation to his peers. When this avoidance mechanism becomes habitual and is prolonged into adult life, it results in impoverishment of the ego.

For centuries the Jewish people avoided situations which were natural to a nation living on its own land, and at the same time they avoided the efforts and obligations such situations entail. This "people of readers" came to specialize almost exclusively in commercial and financial activities and in the exercise of the intellect on religious and moral questions. They lost both the qualities and the defects inherent in "manual" pursuits. They acquired the qualities but also the inadequacies of the intellectual way of life.

IX

And so we perceive that in the formation of the Jewish traits historical development, social conditions and childhood influences all converge toward a renunciation of the use of physical force and violence. Repression and inhibition of physical force may lead to a fixation at one of two stages of psychological development known as "oral sadism" and "anal sadism." Oral sadism may be reinforced in the case of the Jews by the tremendous religious importance attached to the nature and preparation of food, which has strengthened the tendency to focus psychological conflicts arising from other sources on food. Then again we have seen how most of the temporal aspirations of the Jews came to be concentrated on money. It is known that preoccupation with money is stimulated by forces coming from the anal-sadistic stage. Thus the traditional economic life conditions of the Jewish people serve to reinforce the anal-sadistic drives in the life of the individual Jew.

Repression of the aggressive drives may have another result. Aggressions cannot be really eradicated, and when repressed generally react upon the self. They are instrumental in creating guilt feelings and anxiety, and their derivative inhibitions. Anxiety culminating in behavior disturbances of the "whipped dog" type is due to this dislocation in the economy of the aggressive drives. The impact of persecution and the repression of counteraction end by curbing even the volition towards counteraction and transforming it into anxiety.

The historically evolved renunciation of violence as a means of defense against stronger enemies, continual living in conditions in which survival depended upon complete abnegation of physical force, the transmission of these principles through tradition, the intangible dangers to which Jews have always been exposed and against which force would be of no avail—all these factors have converged to produce a strong tendency toward anxiety and an "inferiority complex" in a great many Jews. It is the price they have had to pay for their hard-won survival.

Jewish aggression, deflected from its normal channels, has found outlet in psychological and social channels. The higher incidence of neurosis among Jews is undoubtedly an outcome of this process. It is responsible for personality disturbances such as lack of dignity and self-respect, and for character traits that are built up on that part of the aggressiveness which seeks satisfaction through possession—such as the need to dominate and to impose by one's possessions.

X

If we concede that certain traits are found more frequently in Jews than in non-Jews, can the psychoanalytic method as we have applied it here provide an adequate explanation?

The question might still be asked whether there are not some special "racial" characteristics—apart from social and historical conditioning—based on hereditarily transmitted traits. There is no doubt that in every human being, Jew or non-Jew, there are innate variable predispositions, and that some of these predispositions, but probably not all, are transmitted through heredity. But is it conceivable that in the case of the Jews there may also be a set of hereditarily transmitted predispositions responsible for the special Jewish traits we have described? Until a comparative study of Jewish and non-Jewish infants and young children has been made there is no way of evaluating or validating such a hypothesis.

We must bear in mind that it is not the character

trait itself which is innate, but certain predisposing factors, which do not always necessarily result in the formation of a particular trait in the adult. Identical twins, with the same hereditary predispositions, may develop character traits which on the surface appear very dissimilar but which are shown by psychoanalysis to have a common origin.* Even after an individual has been psychoanalyzed it is usually difficult to discern the components of an isolated trait and to determine to what extent it is based on innate predispositions. The lack of apparent connection between a predisposition and its resulting trait is such that we should beware of deducing the existence of the one from the presence of the other. And this because from the earliest age environment plays such an essential part in the formation of character.

In the case of the Jews, the problem of hereditary predispositions is even further complicated. Those who believe in a "Jewish ethos"—basing their belief on the small amount of modification the Jewish character appears to have undergone during a century and a half of emancipation—should remember that only a very small fraction of the Jewish world population has benefited from the legal emancipation brought about by the French Revolution. Other countries of Western and Central Europe only gradually and partially followed France's example. It is only very recently that the great mass of Jews in the reservoirs of Russia and Poland, which have supplied the major flow of immigrants to America and Western Europe, have known legal emancipation.

* See Heinz Hartmann: Psychiatrische Zwillingsstudien. *Jahrbuch für Psychiatrie.* Wien: Springer, 1934.

We must also bear in mind that there is always a considerable time lag between social or legal changes and their observable effects on psychological make-up. This is due to the preponderant influence on children of their early and enduring identification with their parents and the superego of their parents. Past events in the group history transmitted by tradition and identification from one generation to the next have an influence on individual members of the group that could be mistaken for hereditary transmission of responses.

Another cause for this time lag is that in spite of progressive legal emancipation, anti-Semitism has never disappeared in Europe. We are apt to forget that it takes two or three generations to bring about any perceptible changes. Moreover, a strong argument in favor of the theory that Jewish traits are dependent on psychological factors created by social conditions, rather than on hereditary predispositions, can be found in the radical change in the character of Jews who have been born and raised in Palestine.

Whatever validity there may be in the theory of hereditary predisposition, it is certain that historical and social factors have played and continue to play a preponderant role in the formation of the personality of Jews in the Diaspora.

The question might be raised as to how the psychoanalytic theory that neuroses and personality disturbances are determined by family conflicts can be reconciled with the importance we have attributed to extrafamilial pathogenic conditions in the creations of psychic disorders in Jews. The answer lies in the few remarks on neuroses at the beginning of this chapter.

The psychological conflicts which confront the Jews are fundamentally the same as those which confront their non-Jewish neighbors. But owing to their peculiar social, historical and psychological status, additional conflicts, from which most non-Jews are exempt, are superimposed on these fundamental and universal conflicts.

XI

We have already described the type of neurotic whose behavior unconsciously leads him into distressing situations, and we have seen that one of the underlying mechanisms of this type of behavior is the turning against himself, under pressure of moral forces, of the individual's own inhibited aggressive impulses. The tendency to direct aggressive impulses against the self, which in its exaggerated form may result in disturbances in the economy of the aggressive impulses, as in "moral masochism," is a common one in modern civilized man. However, according to Freud and Waelder, there is a tendency in this day and age to revolt against this psychological end result of the process of our civilization. The National Socialist movement is a case in point. The driving power of the Nazi ideology lay in a return to concepts chief among which was admiration —even worship—of aggressive brute force. We have seen that Nazi hatred of the Jews can be attributed to this regression, since the Jews have carried the repression of aggressive physical force to greater lengths than any other occidental people.

Are we justified in concluding that, since they have this tendency to turn their aggressive drives against themselves after the manner of neurotics who unconsciously desire suffering, the Jews must also unconsciously desire it, even to the point of letting themselves be massacred?

The theory that a man's own unconscious is the master of his fate, and that he who experiences misfortune and failure does so because of his unconscious need to suffer, is based on somewhat sweeping generalizations. The individual is not living in a vacuum, but surrounded by other human beings who also have conscious and unconscious drives. Furthermore, the evolution of man takes place in highly complex conditions, subject to the influence of biological and sociological factors, as well as nonhuman and inanimate factors. Even if the fate of some individual Jews can be explained in terms of their moral masochism, the plight of the Jewish people as a whole cannot be reduced to such a simple psychological mechanism. It is a convenient oversimplification for those who would like to throw responsibility for their mistreatment on the victims themselves. It is not conceivable that the tragic fate of so many human beings can be interpreted in terms of their desire to satisfy an unconscious need for suffering and atonement. Can we bring ourselves to believe that the millions of civilians and soldiers—both Jews and Gentiles—killed during the last war, perished because they were afflicted with moral masochism, and that those who escaped owe their survival to their freedom from this particular neurosis?

Since it would seem probable that repression of physical violence has resulted in an increase in the number of neurotics among Jews, there may be some justification in assuming that a greater number of

Jews than of Gentiles suffer from "moral masochism." On the other hand, Jews also manifest in marked degree the opposite tendency: the will to live and to succeed in life. This is demonstrated by the remarkable facility with which Jews "bounce back" when they get a chance; in fact, this very resilience has been the target of much anti-Jewish criticism. And the fact that they have survived as a group in spite of all the odds against them is proof of their tenacious, stubborn will to live.

There have been various in-group forces of cohesion which have also been potent factors in the survival of the Jewish group. Devout Jews, whether in the Middle Ages or in modern times, have always felt that they had a sacred mission to fulfill: to preserve the one true faith until the coming of the Messiah, who will establish the Law of God on earth for the good of all mankind. Faith in their sacred mission has given them strength to bear the worst persecutions.

Why do Jews who have lost all traditional and religious ties with their people still cling to their Jewishness? Some of them uphold what Bienenfeld calls the "religion of the nonreligious Jews," that is to say, they believe in justice and universal good and deem it their duty to propagate and defend these ideals, not so much as Jews but as citizens of their respective countries. Others again desire only to live a simple life; they do not want to hear of their mission as Jews, they have no desire to be champions of new ideas, they just want to live the lives of ordinary human beings, merged in the life around them. One of the special characteristics of the modern anti-Semitic movement is that it makes such an assimilation extremely difficult. In some rare instances baptism and denial of their Jewish origins is still possible, but many Jews have refused to resort to this measure because they consider it cowardly; so many of their relations and friends have been massacred, or persecuted, or at the least calumniated, that they would have the feeling of condoning these outrages in dissociating themselves from the victims. Others again are repelled by the thought that if they were to become converts their children might at some future date be recruited into the ranks of the anti-Semites.

Some of the psychological sources of internal cohesion may be sought in the strong family bonds formed in early childhood. The extremely precocious religious teaching given to children in devout Jewish families, inculcating total submission to God the Father, is also an important factor in the formation of a deep attachment to the parents and to family traditions. Moreover, in the conditions of life in a persecuted minority, the hostile components of the oedipus complex can very easily be diverted onto the persecutors, and this in turn will strengthen the family attachment. The fact that the Jew has always been considered an outsider, wherever he has lived, and often a diabolical or despicable outsider as well, has made the psychological process of detachment from his family harder for the Jew than for the non-Jew.

Chapter V

ISRAEL AND CHRISTIANITY:
A CULTURAL PAIR

I

Many aspects of the problem of survival have been the same for the Jews as for other national or religious minorities. There are, however, unique and special aspects in the survival of the Jews which distinguish them from all other minorities, and which are to be attributed to the unique relationship that has always existed between the Jewish minority and the surrounding Christian majority. Together, Christians and Jews have always formed a "cultural pair." Indeed, the reason and the result of the Jewish survival can only be explained in terms of this cultural pair. Furthermore, it is this relationship which is at the basis of the conflict which has always both divided and bound together Christians and Jews.

In ancient times, after their military defeat at the hands of powerful enemies, the Jewish people achieved the well-nigh impossible feat of resisting almost overwhelming pressures toward disintegration. Other conquered peoples of that period yielded not only to the military might of their conquerors but also to the prestige of their cultures. The Jews, as we have seen, withstood the latter temptation by means of a special psychological mechanism. They assumed the blame for defeat and interpreted it as a punishment inflicted on them by God for their sins. In psychological terms, this reaction was due to a powerful superego, capable of counterbalancing the importance of instinctual satisfactions. Later, at the time of the Roman conquest, they were again able to survive by choosing a course of nonviolence. And although they succumbed to the tremendous prestige of Greco-Roman civilization to the extent of adopting its languages and customs, on the plane of religion and ethics the Jews remained faithful to their own basic principles.

After the schism between Judaism and Christianity and during the first centuries of the existence of the latter as an independent religion, Christianity regarded Judaism as a dangerous rival. The early Fathers of the Church denounced the Jews as accursed and forsaken by God; and yet at the same time they laid the foundations for the special tolerance Christianity has always manifested toward the Jews.

In the Middle Ages, economic motives for persecuting the Jews were added to the religious ones. Their gradual exclusion from almost all professions except those of usury and related occupations, led to their being singled out for the *opprobrium* of the surrounding peoples. The Jews now bore the stigma of Judas and "dirty money" in addition to the stigma of deicides.

In the nineteenth and twentieth centuries, political and economic motives gradually became the dominant ones in the persecution of Jews. The Tzarist government of Russia instigated pogroms for the deliberate purpose of diverting political and social discontent away from the defects of the existing regime. Political manipulation of anti-Semitism reached its peak in Nazi

Germany. The Nazi leaders used it to serve widely divergent ends: to restore national pride by attributing the German defeat to the Jews; to exalt national vanity and race consciousness by proclaiming Jews an inferior race; to fuse all internal dissensions into a common hatred against an "inner enemy;" to gain a fifth column of supporters and sympathizers in foreign countries; to disguise and dissimulate their own designs for world domination by projecting them onto the "Elders of Zion;" to stifle the forces of conscience and morality in the German people by an indirect attack on Christianity through the Jews. The Jews through the Nazi propaganda became the universal scapegoat and were held responsible for all the ills of the world.

II

In the process of their fight for survival the Jews have acquired certain neurotic traits which have become additional pretexts for persecution. Their fate, however, cannot be explained in terms of these peculiar characteristics. It might be said that the fact that they have survived has made them the "tabooed People" for the Christians—sacred but not holy, dreaded, disturbing, forbidden, impure. But this is not the whole story. They also owe their survival to the fact that they were already the Chosen People and later, in their own Messianic beliefs, the People of the Priests. It was not until much later that they became the "tabooed People" for the Christians.

Not only did they survive with a separate identity, but they perpetuated this identity in the Judaeo-Christian culture, which they helped beget and in which their vital role has been precisely that of the tabooed People. They acquired this special function as a result of unique sociological and historical conditions and of their own peculiar psychological characteristics. With it they won the admiration, as well as the contempt, hatred, fear and envy of their cultural hosts. These ambivalent reactions have in turn left an indelible mark upon the Jews and have reinforced their conviction of being a unique and exceptional group of human beings, set apart from other men.

By having held aloof from such significant social functions as the sharing of a meal, the Jews have exposed themselves to reciprocal exclusions of a much more serious nature. Yet it is precisely this course of isolation and withdrawal that has been largely responsible for their survival. Here we see another link in that strange concatenation of circumstances: the very factors which have enabled them to survive have become sources of hatred and prejudice against them. In the Middle Ages, by holding aloof and remaining foreigners, the Jews became the object of expulsions and migrated, thereby avoiding extermination. They are still treated as foreigners although they abandoned their voluntary isolation long ago. For Christians everywhere, they symbolize the foreigner *par excellence*. The ghetto walls have had a dual function. They have protected the Jews, but they have also made them an ever-available target. The most recent of the ghettos, which the Nazis set up in Warsaw, afforded a particularly good example of the second of these functions.

In the vicious circle created by the interplay of forces engendered by the personality traits of the Jews and the reactions to them of the surrounding peoples, the ghetto is symbolic in another sense also. Armed force, whether used for protection or attack, has always been found on only one side of its walls. The refusal of the Jews to fuse with the surrounding population has condemned them to remain perpetual foreigners, but it has also saved them from extinction. But their way of survival—the preservation of their identity as a group—contained the seeds of all future anti-Semitism.

In short, they have always been persecuted, so it is accepted and acceptable that they always will be. Because they were accursed of God they were driven out, and because they were thus compelled to wander over the face of the earth, the curse seemed to be corroborated. They are hated because they have managed to survive through centuries of persecution, and to survive as a distinct group among the peoples who have both sheltered and persecuted them. Their role in Christian society is what has predestined them throughout history to be the victims of man's cruelty.

III

It is extraordinary that the Jews have become the symbol for so many conflicting and contradictory concepts at one and the same time. Sometimes they are perceived as remote and alien, at other times they seem so closely akin that ways are sought in vain to recognize them. Sometimes they are pictured as alarmingly powerful, sometimes as contemptibly weak. Sometimes they personify evil, sometimes man's conscience. All this interchangeably and even simultaneously.

They are always available and always expendable

in any of the conflicts which assail the human ego.* In the conflict of the ego with external reality, the Jew may be perceived as powerful and threatening, or as weak and contemptible. In the conflict of the ego with the id the Jew may become the symbol of Evil—the instincts man struggles to repress. In the conflict of the ego with the superego, Israel may represent a people who have kept faith with their God through centuries of persecution and suffering, and who have survived despite their weakness, thanks to their high moral qualities. The traditional identification of the Jews with the people of the Bible, with the prophets, with the events described in the Gospels and with Christ himself, leads quite naturally to their being associated with the superego.

IV

The explanation for the many different roles Israel has had in Christian psychological conflicts is to be found in its history, and specifically in its role in Christian culture.

Judaism and the cultures it has influenced—Islam and Christianity—are intimately bound up with each other. Jewish communities in other cultures—in India or China, for example—have either disappeared or remained static. Only in Moslem and Christian countries, where there has been a mutual cultural influence, have they survived and flourished.

Judaism has always stood and will always stand for something quite special and apart in the philosophy of the religions it engendered. Mohammed started

---

* I owe this formulation to Heinz Hartmann.

out by calling on the religious leaders of Israel to join the new religion. Only after they had refused did he incite his followers to hate Judaism. And though they have maintained this hatred to the present day, the Moslems have always considered the Jews the true People of the Book. In the same way, Luther first tried to win the Jews to his cause, and it was only after their refusal to join him that he denounced them.

The miracle of Jewish survival through the persecutions of the Middle Ages is largely due to the tolerant attitude of the Church. The Jews might well symbolize the curse of Cain, but woe to him who touched Cain. When all other means failed to convert them to Christianity, the Popes forbade the use of force. The Jews might be persecuted, but they must not be annihilated. It was essential that they survive as living witnesses of the true Christian faith and keepers of the Holy Writ. When the Jews were expelled from France, they obtained permission to dwell in Avignon, the city of the Popes. And they have always lived in Rome in ghettos, persecuted but tolerated by the Popes.

V

Jewish communities managed to survive behind ghetto walls and emancipated Jews have managed to flourish in Christian cultures for a very good reason—Christianity needed them. This brings us back to our theory that Israel and Christianity—or to put it differently, the Jews and the peoples of the Judaeo-Christian cultures—form a mutually interdependent cultural pair.

Both Jewish and Christian theologians have tried

to explain and define the respective roles of the two protagonists. The Jews have always interpreted their own role in terms of their spiritual mission. There have been various Christian interpretations.

The Gentile world recognized Jehovah, the God of Judah, as their God. Hence the Christian God

> ... made man, is a Jew, the perfect Jew, the Lion of Judah. His mother is a Jewess, the flower of the Jewish race. The apostles were Jews and all the prophets ... (Leon Bloy).

According to Pastor Boegner,

> Israel is not a problem but a dark mystery, and only the Revelation given by God can illuminate it.
> ... We must bring ourselves to acknowledge that the Holy Writ and the Chosen People are inseparably bound together ... How then explain that their existence causes such unbearable difficulties to the peoples of the earth and creates insoluble problems? ... How are we to consider this thorn in the flesh of humanity?

The uniqueness and strangeness of the Jews and the "scandal" of their continued existence among the nations of the earth is explained by the will of God, who has chosen them to be His people and His witnesses. He saved Israel from destruction that it might continue to live as "the eternal shadow of the Church."

> ... Jew and Christian stand face to face like different servants of the one true God, deeply divided yet closely united in the service of one Master. Each bears witness to the other that salvation and damnation depend entirely upon the grace of God, therefore whenever Christians taunt the Jews because God has forsaken them, they are flagrantly mocking the grace of God ... They forget that when Jesus Christ was made man, He took upon

Himself the flesh of a Jew ... They forget that no Christian can share in Christ's pardon *unless he acknowledges the guilt he shares jointly with the Jews for His death** ... Therein lies the solution of the God-given mystery. He who accepts it can no longer hate, or persecute, or condemn the Jews.

The bonds of kinship that exist between Christians and Jews have been described by Maritain in the following way:

> It is no light matter for a Christian to hate or to despise or to humiliate members of the race from which came his God and the Immaculate Mother of his God. That is why the fierce fanaticism of anti-Semitism always turns in the end into fierce fanaticism against Christianity itself.

And in another passage, on the subject of the Passion of Israel: "... in which Christ participates," he writes,

> No one seems aware of the central fact—and by far the most significant from the point of view of the philosophy of history and human destiny—that *the passion of Israel is more and more clearly taking the shape of the Cross.* **

VI

Christian theologians have endeavored to find explanations on a spiritual level for the paradoxes of Christian history. Both have their psychological and historical counterpart. For such statements as "Jews and Christians stand face to face ... deeply divided yet closely united in the service of one Master," or that Israel continues to live "as the eternal shadow of the Church," are but an expression in spiritual terms of

---

* The italics are mine.
** The italics are Maritain's.

our contention that Israel and Christianity form a "cultural pair."

For is it not true that Christianity has been the medium through which the role of Jehovah has expanded from that of tribal God of Judah into the role of God of the universe? Has not the Christian Church, even while persecuting Judaism, ensured its survival? And is it not also a tenet of the Christian religion that "the final goal of all God's ways for man . . . and the ultimate salvation of the world . . . depend on the conversion of Israel (according to the flesh) to Jesus Christ"* The continued existence of the Jews is therefore necessary for the salvation of the Christian world.

VII

Thus it would seem that the basic reason, and the most ancient one, for the Jew's role of scapegoat—and in extension, of usurer, alien, inner enemy—is his participation in the death of Christ and hence in the birth of Christianity. Jesus became Christ only after he was crucified. Through his sufferings on the Cross he took upon himself the sins of all Christians, he became the Savior.

Psychologically speaking, Christians, who benefit by his death, must unconsciously rejoice in it. For it is the very cornerstone of Christianity. Each individual Christian has therefore to deal in some way with the problem of his share of guilt in Christ's death. One way of atonement is through Holy Communion, wherein through identification with Christ the Christian feels

* J. Maritain: *A Christian Looks at the Jewish Question.* New York: Longmans Green & Co., 1939.

prepared to die for love of him. Another way to lessen the burden of guilt is to throw it all on the Jews instead of sharing it jointly with them. The next step is to project onto them also the secret sin of every Christian, of unconsciously rejoicing in Christ's crucifixion. For if, spiritually, Christ is the Redeemer, psychologically he is the divine scapegoat.* And though the Jew may not be a "divine" scapegoat, he is nevertheless in some way sacred and taboo, very near to Christ—Christ's double, almost—and above all a scapegoat whose suffering can be rejoiced in with impunity.

VIII

It may be asked how these historical facts can have had much influence on the people of the present day, most of whom are probably completely ignorant of Jewish history. But history is not only learned from the history books. It is transmitted by word of mouth from generation to generation, together with all the errors and distortions such a method entails. So it has been with the history of the Jews. The traditional concept of the Jew, whether it has been deliberate or unconscious, explicit or implicit, oral or written, has invariably portrayed the Jew as an object of hatred, fear and contempt. The very word "Jew" has become a pejorative noun, with a connotation of danger and hidden mystery.

Tradition may exert its influence at any age. Generally it is at work in early childhood, but sometimes it

* J. Frazer: *The Golden Bough*, Vol. VI. London and New York: Macmillan, 1922.

only makes itself felt in later life. Whether or not anti-Semitic reactions develop in an individual, and the form they take, will depend on his psychopathological tendencies, on his life pattern, and on social conditions.

Furthermore, the idea of the Jews as an available scapegoat has been handed down from generation to generation of Christian youth through the teaching of Bible history, which has been one of the chief means of transmitting and perpetuating in western civilization the cultural pattern, which is the mainspring for all the complex and contradictory roles the Jews have played in the minds of successive generations of Christians.

The Christian child finds in Bible teaching solutions to certain psychological problems that beset all children and which stem from the building up and strengthening of the superego on a conscious level. At this early age the child is just beginning to renounce his unconsciously aggressive attitude towards his father, with its content of unconscious death wishes. The superego is formed by internalizing the moral exigencies of the father, which the son adopts as his own. However, this psychic structure is still incomplete, and religious teaching comes as one of its most powerful reinforcing agents. It offers a spiritual and historical parallel to the child's own father-son conflict. He comes to regard the conflict between Christ and the Jews described in the Bible in terms of his own conflict with his father and of the unconscious death wishes he harbored against him during the oedipal stage. Each succeeding generation of Christian children is offered a possibility of solution to this conflict. As Christians, they can profit by the death of Christ with impunity, throwing the entire load of guilt onto the Jews.

But because the Jews remained faithful to God the Father, they also become the representatives of God in the child's mind. Then they become identified with his own conscience and consequently with his own father, whom he simultaneously admires and loves, and fears and hates. For many Christians, the situation is still more complex. In spite of their conviction that the Jews bear the bloodguilt of Christ's crucifixion, they cannot help perceiving the intimate bonds that bring them close to Christ.

The psychological parallel to the paradox of Israel's position in the Christian world is found in the identification of Jews both with the enemies of Christ and with Christ himself.

It rarely happens that these thoughts rise clearly formulated to the surface of consciousness. Usually they are repressed and are only re-encountered during the process of psychoanalysis. Nevertheless, the factual history of the origins of Christianity, as taught to Christian children, inclines them to regard the Jews as a dedicated people, close to Christ. Without the crucifixion Christianity would not have come into existence, but because of their alleged part in it the Jews carry the burden of guilt and anathema, and though they are essential to Christianity, they must eternally pay the price of this guilt.

> Have they stumbled that they should fall? God forbid; but rather through their fall salvation is come unto the Gentiles . . . For if the casting away of them be the reconciling of the world, what shall their receiving of them be, but life from the dead? (Romans XI:11 and 15).

For all these reasons the Jews have had a unique place in western civilization which has been so radically influenced by Christianity.

Christianity is based on love, charity, and forgiveness of sins. Yet some Christians are convinced that the blood of Christ, allegedly shed by the Jews nineteen centuries ago, is on the head of their descendants to the present day. Judaism is seen as the enemy. Yet it is essential that this enemy survive since the ultimate salvation of the world depends on his conversion. Thus we find that Christian culture is based on two contradictory attitudes toward the Jews. They are the indispensable complement of Christian culture, and notwithstanding, or rather because of this, they are considered the enemy of Christianity.

IX

What has been the extent of the influence on modern anti-Semitism of the factors described above, Bible teaching and traditional mythology, and the extent of the influence of socioeconomic and individual psychological factors? And how have they all interacted to produce the complex phenomenon that is modern anti-Semitism?

In the light of direct observation it might seem that we have attached too much importance to religious factors. If one were to question individual German, French or American anti-Semites, very few would be found who consciously attribute their antagonism to the role the Jews are supposed to have played in the death of Christ. On the other hand, it would probably be easy enough to pick out from behind the various rationalizations the influence of such sociological factors as we have described earlier, especially those of an economic order. Nevertheless, these socioeconomic factors would not be sufficient in themselves to produce such a complex phenomenon if it were not for two other contributory influences which, though they may act upon the individual in entirely different ways, yet stem from the same origin: early religious teaching and tradition.

The importance of religious teaching lies in the fact that it leaves its mark in childhood, before economic factors have entered the picture. It creates an individual pattern in the child, part of which is a feeling of ambivalence towards Jews and the potentiality to make use of them as scapegoats. This is a fundamental characteristic of anti-Semitism, and religious teaching is not by any means the only source in the majority of cases. It is true that there are some cases where it appears to have been the only factor, as in the case of the Japanese students described by Kallen. These boys, educated as Christians, had never known any Jew before coming to an American university. There they became good friends with some Jewish boys, but broke with them on finding out they were Jews. On the other side, of course, there is the case of the Antilles Negroes who led a revolt against their white masters with cries of "Death to the White Men who crucified Jesus!" Obviously in the latter case the religious motive was by no means the only one, and the same is true of the pogroms of the Middle Ages and of modern times.

Furthermore, religious teaching does contain elements of both aspects of the Jew. The orientation it will take in the mind of each child, therefore, depends partly on the way the facts are presented and partly on the psychological make-up of the child.

There are different ways of teaching religious history. One method might stress the guilt of the Jews in the crucifixion and the "sins of the fathers visited upon the children." But religion may also be taught in a spirit that accords to contemporary Jews the pardon wrung from centuries of atonement in suffering and anguish. Then again, no explicit orientation need be given to the young Christian's attitude towards his Jewish fellow men.

It is quite evident that when a child is indoctrinated with the need for avenging the death of Christ on contemporary Jews he will almost inevitably become anti-Semitic. But regardless of what particular slant is given to his religious instruction, the point we wish to make is that its effects will largely be determined by the psychological make-up of the child. It will depend on the respective stages of development of the various components of the oedipus complex, and particularly on the outcome of the conflict between his love and hate feelings for his father: for example, on the degree of intensity of his unconscious death wishes and on the defense mechanisms which a given child sets up to protect himself against his aggressive drives.

We said earlier in the book that the perseveration of a certain form of ambivalence and the tendency to make use of a projection mechanism, whereby one's own unconscious desires are attributed to others, are predisposing factors, or adjuncts of anti-Semitism.

These are but two of the motivating factors which may lead to the crystallization of aggressions against the Jews. For example, environment may be a preponderant factor. A long tradition of anti-Semitism affords the opportunity to any individual in times of stress to concentrate all his aggressions on the Jew. The force of this anti-Jewish tradition will vary in different classes of the population, in different countries and in different periods in history. Not all individuals are necessarily influenced by it. Again, there are certain individuals whose pathological traits turn them into fanatical anti-Semites, and these in turn can wield a powerful influence on their predisposed followers.

The essential point we wish to make is that the imprint left on the individual by tradition has its parallel in the historical evolution of this tradition. The historical role of Israel in the birth of Christianity was the mainspring for all anti-Semitic feelings, which are based psychologically on the same forces activated in children of the contemporary world by the teaching of this history.

Nineteen centuries have passed since the first generation of Christians broke away from Judaism and adopted the religion of God the Son against the religion of God the Father. Both in terms of the individual and in terms of history, this separation involved antipaternal feelings. Christians, denying these antipaternal feelings in themselves, imputed them exclusively to the Jews, so that the Jews alone were charged with killing God. Religious teaching has crystallized the respective functions of Jew and Christian in Judaeo-Christian culture—that of the Jew being to serve as a scapegoat for the Christian, ever available in time of need. Subsequently, special social conditions helped perpetuate this Jewish role in the cultural pattern.

Their dual function—to be branded with infamy but by the same token to be necessary and useful—was the primordial condition for their survival in the Christian world. This dual function took on many new aspects during the course of history. The original Jewish myth was overlaid with new versions which have had an important part in shaping the modern concept of the Jew. Their role of bankers and moneylenders in the Middle Ages, for example, which incurred for them the stigma of usury, became one of the most powerful affective motivations in the modern economic type of anti-Semitism. In the Middle Ages, too, another facet was added to the Jewish myth which has also lasted to the present day: the idea of the Jew as the eternal foreigner, the Wandering Jew without a country, which is based partly on the identification with Judas handed down from the preceding period. All these special attributes superimposed on the original theological concept of the Jew became additional reasons for the role of scapegoat in popular sentiment and in political strategy.

The Jews paid dearly for their survival in another way too. They were forced to adapt themselves not only economically but psychologically to the special conditions of their survival. Centuries of life in ghettos, endless persecutions and expulsions, left their mark on them both psychologically and socially. And in turn, the special personality traits they acquired afforded fresh pretexts for hatred and persecution.

In modern times new themes have been woven into the traditional myth. One of these is the idea that the Jew belongs to a special race. Another is that they are responsible for all the ills and upheavals that beset the modern world, as a counterpart to the important contributions they have made to the intellectual, social and political development of our epoch.

It is evident that the traditional image of the Jew available to modern man is composed of many facets, acquired during the common history of this cultural pair. All are facets added to the original concept evolved at the birth of Christianity. All are an indirect reflection of the Christians' reaction to their moral debt to the Jews. All reflect also Christianity's incomplete victory over Israel.

Chapter VI

OUTLOOK FOR THE FUTURE

Long before the end of World War Two it was easy to foresee that the defeat of Nazi Germany would not put an end to anti-Semitism. On the contrary, it could be expected to continue both in Europe and America. For the Nazis had replenished the store of historical causes that form the permanent stockpile of anti-Semitism. They had broadcast lies which, however fantastic, had obtained credence and would continue to have repercussions throughout the world. They had demonstrated that it was relatively easy to persecute Jews, and even to exterminate them, with impunity. And above all they left in the wake of their defeat an impoverished, ravaged, ruined Europe; a Europe more deeply torn politically than perhaps ever before in her history.

At this hour, in a world divided by the "iron curtain," there are Jews on both sides of the curtain; and on both sides of it hostility towards them is breaking out again, for reasons diametrically opposed: on the one side the Jews may be accused of being in league with the capitalists, on the other with the communists.

Is Zionism the solution? Certainly for the Jews of Palestine it is. For the enmity of the Arabs and the recent fighting are for the first time "normal" in character. But Zionism can never bring a general solution to the problem so long as the great majority of Jews do not live in Palestine. There is even the risk that it may aggravate it in the United States as it has already done in Great Britain.

The great tragedy for the Jews is that their national home is a country of considerable importance, which, since the creation of the Israeli nation, has become a wedge of the western world in the heart of the Arab countries. It is indeed tragic that the vital interests of so many Jews should be in direct conflict with the vital interests of the Arabs, and in addition with the vital strategic interests of the great world powers.

Are there any existing means of fighting the evil that is anti-Semitism?

Legal sanctions would only be effective in a social system based on regimentation of thought, in which case there is the risk that the remedy might be as dangerous for civilization as the disease itself.

Some may draw the conclusion from the present study that anti-Semitism might be eliminated if the transmission of its cultural foundations through religious teaching were to cease. It is hardly necessary to point out that even if this were to be done, the tradition of anti-Semitism would continue to exist. In any case, it is as useless to count on such a cessation as to look for the disappearance of anti-Semitism by means of a mass conversion of all Jews to Christianity in the near future. It is perhaps less unrealistic to hope, however, that Bible history may be taught with a less explicitly anti-Jewish bias. It is possible that eventually such a change might have considerable results.

It is impossible to eradicate from our culture the fundamental traditional elements which form the historical basis for modern anti-Semitism. But we hope that it will not always be impossible to prevent these potentialities from being translated into violent collective outbreaks.

These outbreaks only occur when a country, or a large segment of population, feels that its existence is threatened and when the resultant tensions and aggressions are manipulated by powerful groups for political ends. It is reasonable to hope that in the not too distant future people will come to realize that anti-Semitism is a social disease which ravages not only the Jews but also the Gentile groups who succumb to it, and that the closer the degree of mutual tolerance and co-operation between the cultural pair, Jews and Christians, the richer will be the flowering of their common civilization.

In their fight against anti-Semitism, Christians and Jews must unite therefore in a common cause: the good of mankind. In this fight there are more powerful weapons than reason, but the search for truth will always be an essential part of it. The present work is an attempt to contribute to it.

BIBLIOGRAPHY

ACKERMAN, NATHAN W. and JAHODA, MARIE: The Dynamic Basis of Antisemitic Attitudes. *Psychoanalytic Quarterly*, XVII, 1948.

ALEXANDER, FRANZ: Culture and Personality: A Round Table Discussion. *American Journal of Orthopsychiatry*, VIII, 1938.

ALEXANDER, FRANZ and STAUB, HUGO: *The Criminal, the Judge and the Public.* Transl. by Gregory Zilboorg. Macmillan, New York, 1931.

ANTISEMITISME. *Foi et Vie*, 1938, No. 4.

ASCH, SHOLEM: *The Nazarene.* G. P. Putnam's Sons, New York, 1939.

———— *The Apostle.* G. P. Putnam's Sons, New York, 1943.

———— *One Destiny.* G. P. Putnam's Sons, New York, 1945.

BAK, ROBERT C.: Masochism in Paranoia. *Psychoanalytic Quarterly*, XV, 1946.

BARON, JOSEPH: *Stars and Sand.* The Jewish Publication Society of America, Philadelphia, 1943.

BARON, SALO WITTMANN: *A Social and Religious History of the Jews.* Vols. I, II, III. Columbia University Press, New York, 1937.

BATESON, GREGORY and MEAD, MARGARET: *Balinese Character.* New York Academy of Sciences, New York, 1942.

BEARD, MIRIAM: Anti-Semitism, Product of Economic Myths. See GRAEBER and BRITT.

BENEDICT, RUTH: *The Patterns of Culture.* Houghton Mifflin Co., Boston, 1934.

BERG, MARY: *Warsaw Ghetto, a Diary.* L. B. Fischer, New York, 1945.

BERGE, FRANÇOIS: Personal communication to the author.

BERGSON, HENRI LOUIS: *Des deux sources de la Morale et de la Religion.* F. Alcan, Paris, 1932.

BETTELHEIM, BRUNO: Individual and Mass Behaviour in Extreme Situations. *Journal of Abnormal and Social Psychology,* XXXVIII, 1943.
BIENENFELD, FRANZ RUDOLPH: *The Religion of the Non-Religious Jews.* Museum Press, Ltd., London, 1944.
────── *The Germans and the Jews.* Becker and Warburg, London, 1939.
BLOY, LEON: *Le Salut par les Juifs.* Paris, 1924.
BOAS, FRANZ: *Anthropology and Modern Life.* W. W. Norton & Co., New York, 1928–32.
BOEGNER, MARC: *L'Evangile et le Racisme.* Edition "Je Sers," Paris, 1939.
BONAPARTE, MARIE: *Les Mythes de Guerre.* Imago Publishing Co., London, 1946.
BRAM, JOSEPH: The Social Identity of the Jews. *Transactions of the New York Academy of Sciences,* Section of Anthropology, Series II, Vol. 6, No. 6, March 1944.
BRICKNER, RICHARD M.: *Is Germany Incurable?* J. B. Lippincott Co., Philadelphia, 1943.
BROWN, J. F.: The Origin of the Anti-Semitic Attitude. See GRAEBER and BRITT.
BROWNE, LEWIS: *The Wisdom of Israel.* An Anthology. Random House, New York, 1945.
BRUNHES, JEAN: *Les Races.* Didot, Paris, 1930.
BRUZKUS, J. D.: The Anthropology of the Jewish People. *The Jewish People,* Vol. I. Jewish Encyclopedic Handbooks, New York, 1946.

CASEY, ROBERT P.: Oedipus Motivation in Religious Thought and Fantasy. *Psychiatry,* V, 1942.
────── Religion and Psychoanalysis. *Psychiatry,* VI, 1943.
Catholic Encyclopædia, The: Vol. VIII (Jews and Judaism). The Universal Knowledge Foundation, Inc., New York, 1913.
CLAUDEL, PAUL: *Les Juifs.* Plon, Paris, 1937.
COHEN, A.: *Everyman's Talmud.* J. M. Dent and Sons Ltd., London, 1937.

BIBLIOGRAPHY 205

COHEN, JOSEPH W.: The Jewish Role in Western Culture. See GRAEBER and BRITT.

COON, CARLETON STEVENS: Have the Jews a Racial Identity? See GRAEBER and BRITT.

COUDENHOVE-KALERGI, HEINRICH: *Anti-Semitism Throughout the Ages.* Hutchinson Co., London, 1935.

DEBRÉ, JACQUES: Personal communication to the author.

DIXON, ROLAND B.: *The Racial History of Man.* Charles Scribner's Sons, New York, 1923.

DOLLARD, JOHN et al.: *Frustration and Aggression.* Yale University Press, New Haven, 1945.

DUBNOW, SEMEN M.: *Weltgeschichte des Jüdischen Volkes.* Jüdischer Verlag, Berlin, 1925–29.

Encyclopædia of Religion and Ethics: Vol. VIII (Judaism). New York, 1920.

ERIKSON, ERIK HOMBURGER: Hitler's Imagery and German Youth. *Psychiatry,* V, 1942.

FAURE, ELIE: *Découverte de l'Archipel.* Nouvelle Revue Critique, Paris, 1932.

FEIWEL, RAPHAEL JOSEPH: *L'Anglais, le Juif et l'Arabe en Palestine.* Transl. by Pierre François Caille. Les Editions de France, Paris, 1939.

FENICHEL, OTTO: Psycho-Analysis of Antisemitism. *American Imago,* I, 1940.

FISHBERG, MAURICE: *The Jews: A Study of Race and Environment.* The Walter Scott Publishing Co., London, 1911.

FLUGEL, J. L.: *Man, Morals and Society.* International Universities Press, New York, 1945.

FRANK, LAWRENCE K.: Culture and Personality. See ALEXANDER, FRANZ.

FRANK, WALDO: *The Jew in Our Day* (with an Introduction by Reinhold Niebuhr). Duell, Sloan & Pearce, New York, 1944.

FRAZER, JAMES G.: The Scapegoat. *The Golden Bough,* Vol. 9. Macmillan Co., London and New York, 1922.

FREEMAN, ELLIS: The Motivation of Jew-Gentile Relationships. See GRAEBER and BRITT.

FRENKEL-BRUNSWIK, ELSE and SANFORD, NEWITT R.: The Anti-Semitic Personality. See SIMMEL.

FREUD, ANNA: *The Ego and the Mechanisms of Defence.* International Universities Press, New York, 1946.

FREUD, SIGMUND: *Introductory Lectures on Psycho-Analysis.* (1917) Transl. by Joan Riviere. George Allen & Unwin Ltd., London, 1922.

———— *Totem and Taboo.* (1913) Transl. by A. A. Brill. Moffat, Yard & Co., New York, 1918.

———— *Group Psychology and the Analysis of the Ego.* (1921) Transl. by James Strachey. International Psycho-Analytical Press, London and Vienna, 1922.

———— *The Ego and the Id.* (1923) Transl. by Joan Riviere. Hogarth Press, London, 1927.

———— Some Character Types met with in Psycho-Analytic Work. (1915) Transl. by E. Colburn Mayne. *Collected Papers,* Vol. IV, Hogarth Press, London, 1925.

———— Mourning and Melancholia. (1916) Transl. by Joan Riviere. *Collected Papers,* Vol. IV. Hogarth Press, London, 1925.

———— The 'Uncanny.' (1919) Transl. by Alix Strachey. *Collected Papers,* Vol. IV. Hogarth Press, London, 1925.

———— *The Future of an Illusion.* (1927) Transl. by W. D. Robson-Scott. Liveright Publishing Corporation, New York, 1928.

———— *New Introductory Lectures on Psycho-Analysis.* (1933) Transl. by W. J. H. Spratt. W. W. Norton & Co., New York, 1933.

———— *Civilization and Its Discontents.* (1930) Transl. by Joan Riviere. Hogarth Press, London, 1930.

———— *Moses and Monotheism.* (1939) Transl. by Katherine Jones. Alfred A. Knopf, New York, 1939.

FRIEDRICH, CARL J.: Anti-Semitism: Challenge to Christian Culture. See GRAEBER and BRITT.

FROMM, ERICH: Die Entwicklung des Christus-Dogmas. *Imago,* XVI, 1930.

GOBINEAU, Comte JOSEPH ARTHUR de: Essai sur l'inégalité des races humaines. Paris, E. Figuière, 1917.

GOLDBERG, JACOB A. and MALZBERG, BENJAMIN: Mental Disease Amongst Jews. *Psychiatric Quarterly*, II, 1928.

GORER, GEOFFRY: Themes in Japanese Culture. *Transactions of the New York Academy of Sciences*, 1942.

GRAEBER, ISACQUE AND BRITT, STUART HENDERSON et al.: *Jews in a Gentile World*. Macmillan Co., New York, 1942.

GRAETZ, HEINRICH H.: *Popular History of the Jews*. Vols. I, II. Jordan Publishing Co., New York, 1935.

GRAYSEL, SOLOMON: *The Church and the Jews in the Thirteenth Century*. The Dropsie College for Hebrew and Cognate Learning, Philadelphia, 1933.

GUIGNEBERT, CHARLES ALFRED HONORE: *Le Monde Juif vers le temps de Jésus*. (*L'Evolution de l'Humanité*) La Renaissance du Livre, Paris, 1935.

HALL, DOROTHY E.: Culture and Personality. See ALEXANDER, FRANZ.

HARTMANN, HEINZ: Psychoanalysis and Sociology. In Lorand, S. (Editor), *Psychoanalysis Today*. International Universities Press, New York, 1945.

———— Psychiatrische Zwillingsstudien. *Jahrbuch für Psychiatrie*. Springer, Wien, 1934.

HARTMANN, HEINZ and KRIS, ERNST: The Genetic Approach in Psychoanalysis. *The Psychoanalytic Study of the Child*, Vol. I. International Universities Press, New York, 1946.

HARTMANN, HEINZ, KRIS, ERNST and LOEWENSTEIN, RUDOLPH M.: Notes on the Theory of Aggression. *The Psychoanalytic Study of the Child*, Vol. III, IV. International Universities Press, New York, 1949.

HERSCH, LIEBMAN: *Le Juif délinquant*. Alcan, Paris, 1938.

HERTZLER, JOYCE O.: The Sociology of Anti-Semitism Through History. See GRAEBER and BRITT.

HOOTON, ERNEST ALBERT: *Apes, Men and Morons*. G. P. Putnam's Sons, New York, 1937.

———— *Twilight of Man*. G. P. Putnam's Sons, New York, 1939.

HORKHEIMER, MAX: Sociological Background of the Psychoanalytic Approach. See SIMMEL.
HUXLEY, JULIAN: *Uniqueness of Man.* Chatto & Windus, London, 1941.

JACOBS, MELVILLE: Jewish Blood and Culture. See GRAEBER and BRITT.
Jewish Encyclopædia: Vol. VII (Judaism). Funk and Wagnalls, New York and London, 1901–1906.
JONES, ERNEST: The Psychology of Religion. In Lorand, S. (Editor), *Psychoanalysis Today.* International Universities Press, New York, 1945.
——— Gentile and Jew. See NEWMAN.

KAHLER, ERICH: *Israel unter den Völkern.* Humanitas Verlag, Zürich, 1936.
KALLEN, HORACE: National Solidarity and the Jewish Minority. *The Annals of the American Academy of Political and Social Science,* Philadelphia, September 1942.
——— *Judaism at Bay. Essays Toward the Adjustment of Judaism to Modernity.* Bloch Publishing Co., New York, 1932.
KARDINER, ABRAHAM: *The Individual and His Society.* Columbia University Press, New York, 1939.
——— *The Psychological Frontiers of Society.* Columbia University Press, New York, 1945.
KASTEIN, JOSEPH: *History and Destiny of the Jews.* Garden City Publishing Co., New York, 1936.
KAUTSKY, KARL: *Der Ursprung des Christentums.* I. H. W. Dietz, Stuttgart, 1910.
KECSKEMETI, J. and LEITES, N.: Some Psychological Hypotheses on Nazi Germany. *Experimental Division for the Study of War Time Communications;* Harold D. Lasswell, Chief. Doc. No. 60, July 30, 1945.
KERILLIS, HENRI de: *Français, voici la vérité.* Editions de la Maison française, New York, 1942.
KLAUSNER, JOSEPH: *Jesus of Nazareth.* Macmillan Co., New York, 1925.

―――― *From Jesus to Paul*. Macmillan Co., New York, 1943.
KLINEBERG, OTTO: *Social Psychology*. Henry Holt & Co., New York, 1937.
KNIGHT, ROBERT P.: Anti-Jewishness and Anti-Semitism. *T.P.R.*, Vol. VI, No. 21, October 19, 1949. The Menninger Clinic, Topeka, Kansas.
KRIS, ERNST: The Danger of Propaganda. *American Imago*, II, 1941.
―――― Mass Communication under Totalitarian Governments. In Waples, Douglas A. (editor), *Print, Radio and Film in a Democracy*, University of Chicago Press, Chicago, 1942.
―――― The Covenant of the Gangsters. *Journal of Criminal Psychopathology*, IV, 1943.
―――― Distrust and Social Change. Paper read at the Eastern Sociological Association, New York, 1943.
―――― Notes on the Psychology of Prejudice. *The English Journal*, Chicago, 1946.
KRIS, ERNST and SPEIER, HANS: *German Radio Propaganda. Report on Home Broadcasts During the War*. Oxford University Press, New York, 1944.
KURTH, GERTRUD M.: The Jew and Adolf Hitler. *Psychoanalytic Quarterly*, XVI, 1947.

LA FARGE, JOHN S.: Anti-Semitism. *Religious Education*, March–April, 1944.
LAGACHE, DANIEL: Le Deuil. *Revue française de Psychanalyse*, X, 1938.
LASSERRE, DAVID: L'Antisémitisme et l'Eglise chrétienne. *Les Cahiers protestants*, 23ème année, No. 1.
LASSWELL, HAROLD D.: The Psychology of Hitlerism. *Political Quarterly*, London, 1933.
LAZARE, BERNARD: *L'Antisémitisme: son histoire et ses causes*. Léon Chailley, Paris, 1894.
LE BON, GUSTAVE: *Psychologie des Foules*. Flammarion, Paris.
LEITES, N.: See KECSKEMETI.
―――― Psycho-Cultural Hypotheses about Political Acts. *World Politics*, 1948.

LEROY-BEAULIEU, ANATOLE: *Israel et l'Antisémitisme.* Reprinted in Rand School of Social Science, New York, 1943.

LINTON, RALPH: *The Cultural Background of Personality.* D. Appleton Century Co., New York and London, 1945.

LODS, ADOLPHE: *Israel, des Origines au milieu du VIIIe siècle. (L'Evolution de l'Humanité.)* La Renaissance du Livre, Paris, 1930.

LOEWENSTEIN, RUDOLPH M.: Origine du Masochisme et la Théorie des Pulsions. *Revue française de Psychanalyse,* X, 1938.

——— The Vital or Somatic Drives. *International Journal of Psycho-Analysis,* XXI, 1940.

——— Historical and Cultural Roots of Anti-Semitism. In Roheim, G. (Editor), *Psychoanalysis and the Social Sciences,* Vol. I. International Universities Press, New York, 1947.

LOWENFELD, HENRY: Some Aspects of a Compulsion Neurosis in a Changing Civilization. *Psychoanalytic Quarterly,* XIII, 1944.

MALLER, JULIUS B.: Juvenile Delinquency among the Jews. *Social Forces,* X, May 1932.

MALZBERG, B.: Prevalence of Mental Disease amongst Jews. See GOLDBERG.

MARITAIN, JACQUES: *La pensée de Saint Paul.* Editions de la Maison française, New York, 1941.

——— *Christianisme et Démocratie.* Editions de la Maison française, New York, 1942.

——— *A Christian Looks at the Jewish Question.* Longmans Green & Co., New York and Toronto, 1939.

——— Preface to OESTERREICHER.

MAYER, CARL: Religious and Political Aspects of Anti-Judaism. See GRAEBER and BRITT.

MEAD, MARGARET: *Cooperation and Competition Among Primitive Peoples.* McGraw-Hill, New York, 1937.

——— *Balinese Character.* See BATESON.

MENNINGER, KARL: *Man Against Himself.* Harcourt & Brace, New York, 1938.

MOELLENDORF, FRITZ: A Projection Returns and Materializes. *American Imago*, III, 1942.

MOORE, GEORGE FOOT: *Judaism in the First Centuries of the Christian Era*. Harvard University Press, Cambridge, 1930–32.

MUHLSTEIN, ANATOLE: Quo Vadis Israel? *La Renaissance*, Vols. II and III, New York, Ecole Libre des Hautes Etudes (New School for Social Research), 1945.

NEUMANN, FRANZ: *Leviathan*. Oxford University Press, New York, 1942.

NEUVILLE, H.: Peuples ou Races. *Encyclopédie Française*, Vol. VII (L'Espèce humaine). Librairie Larousse, Paris.

NEWMAN, CHAIM: *Gentile and Jew*. A Symposium. Alliance Press, London, 1946.

ODIER, CHARLES: Le Complexe du petit profit. *Revue française de Psychanalyse*, V, 1932.

OESTERREICHER, JOHN M.: *Racisme-Antisémitisme-Antichristianisme. Documents et Critiques*. Préface de J. Maritain. Editions de la Maison française, New York, 1943.

ORLANSKY, HAROLD: The Study of Man. Jewish Personality Traits. *Commentary*, II, October 1946.

PARKES, JAMES W.: *The Conflict of the Church and the Synagogues*. Soncino Press, London, 1934.

──────── *The Jew in the Medieval Community*. Soncino Press, London, 1938.

PARSONS, TALCOTT: The Sociology of Modern Anti-Semitism. See GRAEBER and BRITT.

PEGUY, CHARLES PIERRE: Affaire Dreyfus. *Cahiers de la Quinzaine*, Série 4, Cahiers 18, 20. Paris, 1903.

──────── *Notre Jeunesse*. Editions de la Nouvelle Revue Française. Gallimard, Paris, 1933.

PINSKER, LEV S.: *Auto-Emancipation*. Masada Zionist Youth Organization, New York, 1935.

PITTARD, JEAN: *Les Races et l'histoire*. (*L'Evolution de l'Humanité*.) La Renaissance du Livre, Paris, 1930.

REIK, THEODOR: *Der eigene und der fremde Gott.* Internationaler Psychoanalytischer Verlag, Wien, 1923. (English translation in preparation: International Universities Press, New York, 1951.)

REINACH, T.: *Histoire des Israélites.* Hachette, Paris, 1901.

RENAN, E.: *Discours et Conférences,* 7th ed. Calmann-Lévy, Paris, 1922.

—————— *La Vie de Jésus.* Calmann-Lévy, 22nd ed. Paris, 1893.

ROHEIM, GEZA: *The Origin and Function of Culture.* Nervous and Mental Disease Monographs, No. 69. New York, 1943.

ROLLIN, HENRI: *L'Apocalypse de notre temps.* Gallimard, Paris, 1936.

ROTH, CECIL: *The Jewish Contribution to Civilization.* Harper & Brothers, New York and London, 1940.

RUPPIN, ARTHUR: *The Jews of Today.* Henry Holt & Co., New York, 1913.

—————— *Die soziale Struktur des Juden.* Jüdischer Verlag, Berlin, 1930.

RUSSELL, BERTRAND: *A History of Western Philosophy.* Simon & Schuster, New York, 1945.

SACHS, HANNS: Personal communication to the author.

SARTRE, JEAN-PAUL: *Réflexions sur la question juive.* Paul Morihien, Paris, 1946.

SAUSSURE, RAYMOND de: L'Inconnu chez Hitler. *Les Oeuvres Nouvelles.* Editions de la Maison française, New York, 1942.

SIMMEL, ERNST (Ed.): *Anti-Semitism: A Social Disease.* International Universities Press, New York, 1946.

SMITH, WILLIAM BENJAMIN: *Der vorchristliche Jesus.* A. Topelmann, Giessen, 1906.

SOMBART, WERNER: *The Jews and Modern Capitalism.* Transl. with notes by M. Epstein. T. F. Unwin, London, 1913.

STATISTICS OF CRIMINALITY: Publ. by American Jewish Congress, New York City, 1940.

STONEQUIST, EVERETT V.: *The Marginal Man.* Charles Scribner's Sons, New York and Chicago, 1937.

———— The Marginal Character of the Jews. See GRAEBER and BRITT.

TARACHOW, SIDNEY: A Note on Anti-Semitism. *Psychiatry,* IX, 1946.

TARDE, G.: *Les Lois de l'Imitation.* Paris.

TOYNBEE, ARNOLD J.: *A Study of History.* Oxford University Press; Vols. 1, 2, 3, 1933; Vols. 4, 5, 6, 1939.

TRACHTENBERG, JOSHUA: *The Devil and the Jews.* Yale University Press, New Haven, 1943.

VALENTIN, HUGO: *Antisemitism Historically and Critically Examined.* Transl. by Arthur G. Chatev. Viking Press, New York, 1936.

WAELDER, ROBERT: L'esprit, l'éthique et la guerre. Institut de Coopération Internationale. *Coll. correspondances,* Vol. 3, 1934.

———— Aetiologie und Verlauf der Massenpsychosen. *Imago.* XXI, 1935.

———— Notes on Prejudice. *Vassar Alumni Magazine,* May 1949.

WASSERMANN, JACOB: *Mein Weg als Deutscher und Jude.* S. Fischer, Berlin, 1921.

WECHSLER, I. S.: *The Neurologist's Point of View.* L. B. Fischer, New York, 1945.

ZILBOORG, GREGORY: Psychopathology of Social Prejudice. *Psychoanalytic Quarterly,* XVI, 1947.

ZWEIG, ARNOLD: *Die Aufgabe des Judentums.* Verlag des Europäischen Merkur, Paris, 1933.

ZWEIG, STEFAN: *The World of Yesterday.* Viking Press, New York, 1943.

INDEX

Aberration, psychic, 15
Accusations, contradictory, 107
    uniformity of, 13
Ackerman, Nathan, 36, 203
Admiral Kotlchak, 60
"Age of reason," 38
Aggression, 32, 35, 48, 51, 56, 63, 66, 89, 103, 105, 169 et seq., 197
    against God, 162
    inhibition of, 164
    latent, 50, 57
    outlet for, 170
    repression of, 31, 78, 114 f., 135, 164, 173, 177
    transformation of, 164
    turned against the self, 177
Agnostics, 116
Agoraphobia, 17
Agriculture, 59, 80, 117, 171
Ahasuerus, the Wandering Jew, 45
Ambivalence, 27 f., 31, 35, 41 f., 74, 79, 94, 97 ff., 101, 125, 147, 150, 195 f.
Anti-Christianism, 102 et seq.
Anti-Negro reactions, 74
Antipathy, "racial," 20
Antiquity, 43, 74, 80, 181
Anti-Semites, and neurotics, 17 f.
    and psychotics, 16
    fanatical, 34 f., 43, 71, 197
    female, 19
    gullibility of, 63
    inaccessibility to reason of, 18
    in psychoanalysis, 26 et seq., 72
    mentality of, 21
    sexual jealousy of, 72
    superstitions of, 44 et seq.
Anti-Semitic reactions, psychological structure of, 35 et seq.
Anti-Semitism, and envy (jealousy), 21
    and mental illness, 14 et seq.
    and paranoid traits, 15
    and personality traits, 36

Anti-Semitism (continued)
    and self-interests, 21, 24, 105
    and psychological development, 12, 196 f.
    as a political weapon, 13, 53, 64
    as social phenomenon, 49
    as solution to social ills, 18
    anti-Christian, of Nazis, 103 et seq.
    collective, 44, 51
    collective outbreaks of, 49, 58, 202
    criminal, 19
    definition of, 14
    "delusional" or "paranoid," 17 f., 80
    developmental stages of, 30
    diagnosis of, 14
    disappearance of in analysis, 42
    economic, 65, 79 et seq., 182, 195, 198
    epidemics of, 43
    explanation of, 13
    factors in spread of, 44, 101
    fight against, 201 f.
    flare-ups of, 44 et seq., 76, 101
    function of, 25, 49, 105
    fundamental characteristics of, 195
    German, 55, 86, 103 et seq. 177, 183, 200
    historical basis of, 43, 200 ff.
    history of, 13, 120, *et passim*
    in antiquity, 74
    in Middle Ages, 103 f.
    interplay of religious and economic factors, 100
    latent, 59
    medieval, comparison with Nazi, 103 f.
    modern, 75, 77, 120, 179, 194 f., 202
    motives of, 64 et seq.
    obligatory, 58
    of Jews, 133, 144 ff.

INDEX

Anti-Semitism (continued)
  of recent converts, 104, 145, 180
  "pathological," 18
  political manipulation of, 18, 51, 53 et seq., 79, 182, 202
  rationalizations of, 195
  religious, 65, 89 et seq., 99
  sexual factor in, 72
  snobbish type of, 50
  solution to problem, 200 ff.
  symptoms of, 14
  terror of, 144
  types of, 19 f., 64 et seq.
  unconscious, 36, 64
  xenophobic, 64, 78
Anxiety, 108, 131, 142, 173
  reactions, 136
  states of, 15, 137
Apocalypitc age, 94
Arabs, 84, 134, 138, 168, 200 f.
Argentine, 121
Armenians, 69
Aryan race, 56, 69, 103
Asceticism, 39
Asch, Sholem, 142, 203
Assimilation, 54, 67, 76, 86, 111, 115 ff., 143 f., 149, 151, 180
Austria, 61, 75, 87, 116
Avicebron, 84
Avoidance, 169, 172

Babylonian captivity, 70, 162
Bak, Robert C., 34, 203
Baptism, of Jews, 151, 180
Bar Kocheba, 70, 93
Baron, Joseph, 76, 82, 91, 93, 103, 123, 203
Bateson, Gregory, 133, 203
Behavior disturbances, 173
Bergmann, Ernst, 102
Bible, history, 37, 40, 92, 192, 201
Bienenfeld, F. R., 179, 204
Birth rate, of Jews, 115 ff.
Black Plague, 44, 60
Blood groups, 71 f.
Bloy, Leon, 188, 204
Boegner, Marc, 188, 204
Bonaparte, Marie, 11, 57, 88, 204
Brickner, Richard, 15, 204
Bruzkus, J. D., 72, 204

Campaign, anti-Semitic, 11, 19, 56
Canaanites, 70
Canonical laws, 81, 96
Capitalism, 62, 80, 85, 88, 111, 200
Casey, Robert P., 9, 204
Castration complex, 109
Catholic Church, 50, 81 f., 86, 96 f., 158, 190
  protection and tolerance of Jews by, 97 f., 101, 182, 187
Catholics, catholicism, 90, 93, 101, 122, 135
Chamberlain, Houston, 60
Character, diversity of, 117
  formation of, 121, 175
Character neurosis, 132 f.
Character traits, origin of, 174 ff.
Charlemagne, 83
Child-rearing patterns, 133 f.
China, 186
Choice of profession, among Jews, 122 f.
Chosen People, 100, 138, 157, 166, 183, 188
Christ, 37 f., 91, 105, 166
  and the Jews, 37 f., 40 f., 45, 94
  identification with, 40, 142, 190
  the divine scapegoat, 191
  unconscious revolt against, 105
Christianity, 41, 45, 76, 82, 84, 90 et seq., 102, 142, 165 ff., 190
  need of Jews, 187
  origins of, 93 et seq., 193
  role of Christ's death in, 41, 190, 193
Christian Jews, 76, 84
Christianization, 96, 101
Christians and Jews, a cultural pair, 13, 181 et seq., 202
  basis of conflict between, 181
  definition of respective roles, 188 f.
Christians, early, 90, 92
  monophysite, 68
Church Fathers, 94 f., 100, 182
Circumcision, 34, 72, 134
Citizenship rights, 74, 96, 136
Civilization, development of, 104 f.
Claustrophobia, 17
Codet, Henri, 87
Collective ideals, 65 f., 113
Commerce, 80, 82, 172

INDEX   217

Communism, 62, 111, 200
Community, impact of, 153
Comparative studies, methodology of, 121 f.
  of Germans and Jews, 112 ff.
  of maternal attitude, 134
Compulsive neurosis, 114, 164
Conflict(s), and personality traits, 107
  basic, of Jews, 164 f.
  between Christ and Jews, 40, 192
  between young and parent religion, 98, 167, 182
  cultural, 149 ff.
  in childhood, 27, 41
  intrasystemic, 186
  involving family, 26, 151, 176
  of latency period, 38
  provocation of, 107
  repression of, 150
  solutions of, 26 f., 151, 164, 192
  sublimation of, 150
  superimposed on universal, 177
  universal, 177
Constitutio pro Judeis, 97
Conversion, 70, 76, 96, 98, 116, 190, 194, 201
Cosmopolitanism, 55, 151
Crime rate, among immigrants, 151
  among Jews, 121, 126 et seq., 135, 152
Crossbreeding, 68 ff.
Crucifixion, Jew guilt of, 97, 190 f., 193, 196
  psychological meaning of, 41, 193
Cultural lag, 88

Dark Ages, see Antiquity
Debré, Jacques, 110, 205
Defense mechanism, 29 f., 36, 109, 115, 196
Defensive reactions, 121, 145, 147
Deification, of state and race, 104
Delusional system, 61
Delusions, 16
  about Jews, 24, 49
  among anti-Semites, 33
  of persecution, 16, 141
Democracies, hostility to Nazis, 61, 102
  Jew-ridden, 56
Demonopathy, 15

Destruction, of cultural heritage, 104
Deutschreligion, 102
Development, psychological, 27, 29, 38, 172 f.
Dialogue in Hell between Montesquieu and Machiavelli, 60
Diaspora, 92, 168 f., 176
Dictatorship, Judaeo-Masonic, 59
Discrimination, 64, 75, 119
Dispersion, 75, 143, 156
Displacement, 32, 51, 88 f., 105
Drive(s), aggressive, 31 ff., 40, 47, 109, 170 ff., 177
  anal-sadistic, 173
  economy of, 105, 171, 173, 177
  instinctual, 39, 48, 105
  of self-preservation, 89, 170
  sexual, 38
  unconscious, 178

Eastern Europe, 77, 116 f., 118 f., 125, 135 f., 143, 168
Economic competition, 79 et seq.
Economics, laws of, 89
Ego, 27, 29, 104, 109, 136, 172, 186
Egyptians, 70
Einstein, Albert, 23
Elders of Zion, 47, 59, 62, 183
Emancipation, 75 f., 125, 175 f.
England, 115 f., 123, 146, 201
Equality, among Jews, 119
  breakdown of, 81
Equilibrium, emotional, 171
  of group, 52
Erikson, Erik H., 15, 54 f., 140, 205
Ethics, Christian, 142
Ethnico-religious unity, 75, 91
Ethos, Jewish, 175
Evolution, biological and sociological factors in, 178
"Exceptional" status, 147, 153, 156, 184
  genesis of, 160
Expulsion, of evil, 57
Externalization, of unconscious desires, 52

Fanaticism, 189
  of recently converted, 96
  religious, 13, 89 et seq.
Fascism, 78

INDEX

Feiwel, R. J., 82, 84, 205
Fixations, 33, 109, 172
Folklore, 89, 170
Ford, Henry, 60
Food laws, 76
Foreigners, hostility to, 65 et seq., 77 f., 120
"Fossil remnants," 68, 147
France, Frenchmen, 20, 46, 66, 75 f., 87, 116, 122, 132, 146, 158, 175, 187, 194
Frazer, James G., 57, 191, 205
Freemasonry, 62
Freethinkers, 116
Frenkel-Brunswick, Else, 36, 206
Freud, Anna, 144, 172, 206
Freud, Sigmund, 23, 29, 36 f., 48, 51, 65, 101, 104 f., 132, 138, 154, 156, 158, 160, 163, 177, 206

Galicia, 115, 118
General Ludendorff, 60
Germans, 15 f., 53 et seq., 63, 73, 112 f., 122
  Jew-tainted, 56
  "narrow," 54 f.
  national pride of, 53
  Transylvanian, 72
  types of, 54
  "wide," 54
Germany, 86 f., 123, 194
Ghetto, 23, 75, 85, 121, 169, 184 f., 187, 198
God, archaic aspects of, 100
  faith in, 39
  interiorized, 166
  submission to, 37, 99, 180
  universal, 90, 163, 190
Goldberg, Nathan, 127
Gorer, Geoffrey, 129, 207
Gospel, 40, 93, 99, 103, 186
Graves, Mr., 60
Greco-Roman civilization, 92 f., 147, 168, 182
Greek (or Russian) orthodoxy, 90
Greeks, 70, 74, 80, 84, 92
Gregory the Great, 97
Group, aggressions of, 49 f., 88, 202
  dominant, 149 f.
  evolution of, 154
  ideals, 52, 113, 122
  phenomena, 52

Group (continued)
  psychology, 89
  psychopathology, 43 et seq.
Guignebert, C. A. H., 92, 207
Guilt, (sense, feelings of) 22, 34, 37, 39, 46, 55, 63, 106, 157 f., 164, 173, 190 f.
  "borrowed," 159
  shared by Christians with Jews, 189, 191
  unconscious, 108

Haganah, 23
Hallucinations, 61
Hartmann, Heinz, 9, 105, 175, 186, 207
Hebrew (language), 77, 80, 102, 117
Hersch, Leibman, 126, 207
Hillel the Great, 91, 167
Hitler, 12, 50, 54 et seq., 60 et seq., 73 f., 79, 105, 116
  anti-Semitic laws of, 50, 73 f., 85, 104
Hittites, 69
Hooton, E. A., 69, 138, 207
Horkheimer, Max, 86, 208
Humanism, 102
Hungary, 61, 72, 121
Hypochondriasis, 132

Ibn Gabirol, see Avicebron
Id, 29, 186
Identification, 31, 33, 39, 45, 49, 78, 155, 170, 176
  conflicting, 152
  in group formation, 48 f.
  mutual, 48
  of Christ with Israel, 105, 186, 193
  of Jews with Cain, 45
  of Jews with capitalism, 62
  of Jews with devil, 100, 186
  of Jews with enemies of Christ and Christ, 193
  of Jews with Judas, 45, 198
  of property with self, 89
  with a cause, 137
  with heroes, 33, 56, 170
  with Jews, 66
  with the aggressor, 144, 146, 152
  with the dominant group, 152
  with the persecuted, 120, 136

INDEX

India, 186
"Inferiority complex," 55, 142, 146, 173
Inferiority feelings, 118, 132, 140, 146, 149, 156
In-group, aggression, 48, 78
   antagonism, of Jews, 113, 118 f.
   cohesion, 179 f.
"Inner enemy," 56 f., 100, 183, 190
Innocent III, 97
Insanity rate, among Jews, 122, 130 et seq.
Instincts, see also Drives
   cruel, 19
   defense against, 27, 57
   repression of, 41, 135
Internationalization, of aggression, 162
   of parental taboos, 29
   of persecutions, 168
Intolerance of monotheistic religions, 99
   religious, 90
Irgun, 23
Iron curtain, 200
Islam, 84, 90, 186
Isolation, of Jews, 169
   psychological, 168
   spiritual and cultural, 141, 143 f., 184
Israel, see also Jews, Judaism
   and Christianity, a cultural pair, 181 et seq.
   in Christian psychological conflict, 186
   in Christian religion, 43, 94
   passion of, 189
Italy, 71, 76, 78

Jahoda, Marie, 36
Japanese, 129, 195
Jehovah, evolution of concept of, 91
Jerusalem, fall of, 81, 160 f.
Jesus, see Christ
Jewishness, clinging to, 147, 179 f.
Jewish state, destruction of, 96
Jewish territory, autonomous, 14
Jewish vice, 56
Jewry, international, 62
Jews adaptation to host countries, 55

Jews (continued)
   admiration of Christians, 142
   agnostic, 116 f.
   American, 119 f.
   anthropological studies, 69
   as eternal exiles, 79, 198
   as eternal foreigners, 184, 198
   as "living witnesses of true Christian faith," 45, 98 f., 187
   as murderers of Christ, 37, 40, 189, 194
   as "nomadic" people, 46
   as scapegoat, 11, 34, 36 f., 40, 57, 106, 183, 190 f., 195, 198
   as sexual pervert, 72
   as witnesses of God, 188
   assimilated, 119
   attitude toward Christians, 142 ff.
   attitude toward themselves, 142 et seq.
   attraction to and repulsion of, 20, 72, 166, 187 et seq.
   baiters, 49, 137
   characteristics of, 69 ff., 78, 107 et seq., 169
   chauvinism of, 118, 146
   concentration in liberal professions, 87
   consciousness, 44, 78
   contradictory criticism of, 110 f., 185
   critical insight of, 56, 140
   desire for homeland, 167
   diabolical (mythical), 46, 180
   dissimilar groups of, 117 ff.
   distrust of Christians, 141 et seq.
   dual attitude toward, 95, 183 et seq.
   dual function of, 198
   Dutch, 116
   economic status of, 122 ff.
   effects on other nations, 14
   freethinking, 115 f.
   French, 54, 66, 71, 116, 119 f., 158
   German, 54, 71, 112, 118 f.
   "good" and "bad," 20
   hellenized, 93
   history of, 70, 77, 80 et seq., 160 et seq., 191
   homogeneous group of, 117, 123
   identification with fellow Jews, 120 f., 144

INDEX

Jews (continued)
  in antiquity, 70, 74, 80 et seq., 91 et seq., 138, 160 et seq, 181
  individualism of, 118
  in history of Christianity, 41, 100, 156, 197
  in Middle Ages, 83, 96, 167 et seq., 179, 182, 184, 198
  in modern era, 85 et seq., 179, 182, 199
  Italian, 54
  lack of country, 79, 143
  liberal-religious, 115
  loss of homeland, 14, 160 f.
  manners of, 129 f.
  mythical concept of, 46 f., 117
  nationalistic, 119
  nation of, 14, 77
  on equal footing with host nation, 128, 141
  origin of, 69 f., 147 f.
  orthodox, 114 ff., 119, 129, 132, 168
  Palestinian, 93, 138, 176
  personifying evil, 57
  Polish, 71, 119, 126
  psychoanalysis of, 153 et seq.
  psychological make-up of, 107, 155
  reactions to injustice, 159 f.
  rehabilitation of, 125, 130
  religious, 129, 134
  resisting Christianization, 97, 101, 167, 187
  role as usurers, 45
  role in Christian society, 185 f., 192
  Ruppin's division of, 115 f.
  Russian, 71, 86, 119
  self-consciousness of, 78
  special talents of, 123 f.
  spiritual nation of, 14
  superstitions about, 44 et seq.
  survival of, 101, 144, 148, 161, 163, 166, 173 f., 179, 181, 183 f., 186 ff., 198
  "tabooed people," 45 f., 166, 183 f.
  temporal problems of, 165
  theological concept of, 45, 189 ff.
  traditional concept of, 43, 55, 191, 199

Jews (continued)
  traditional prizing of knowledge, 124, 135
  unique status of, 143, 184
Joly, Maurice, 60
Judaeo-Christian interdependence, 187
Judaeo-Christian relations, history of, 95 et seq.
Judaeophobia, 15, 17 et seq.
Judaism and Christianity, bond between, 142, 187 et seq.
  schism between, 91 et seq., 165, 182, 197
Judaism, 70, 77, 90 et seq., 102, 162, 165 ff.
  and Islam, 186 f.
  ethics of, 100
  fundamental laws of, 75
  international, 103
  leaders of, 59, 70, 75, 167 f., 187
  meaning of for Jews, 77
  sects of, 128, 168
  traditions of, 95

Kallen, Horace M., 9, 195, 208
Kecskemeti, J., 114, 208 f.
Klausner, Joseph, 92, 142, 208
Kris, Ernst, 9, 52, 58, 207, 209
Kurth, G., 74, 209

Lasserre, David, 97, 209
Latency period, 38, 40
Lazare, Bernard, 120, 209
Leader-group relationship, 48, 50
Leites, Nathan, 58, 114, 208 f.
Lenin, 61
Libido, development of, 109
Lombardians, 84
Loucheur, M., 87
Love object, forbidden, 73
Lower clergy, 97
Luther, 101, 187

Maccabeans, 165, 170
Maimonides, 84, 168
Manic-depressive psychosis, 131
Mankind, destruction of, 61
  psychic life of, 14

INDEX

Mannerisms, Jewish, 20
Marginal man, 147 et seq.
Maritain, Jacques, 102, 189 f., 210
Marriage laws, 70, 73
Marriages, mixed, 116
Marvaud, Angel, 118
Masochism, 34, 55
  moral, 177 ff.
Mass aggression, 47, 58, 77
"Master race," 56, 62, 104 f.
Materialism, 111
Mead, Margaret, 133, 203, 210
Mechanisms, generating aggression, 47
  psychological, 27, 49, 108, 157, 164, 168, 178, 181
Mediterranean Basin, 70
"Mental contagion," 44, 48
Mental diseases, 130 et seq.
  social, 19, 49
Mentality, Jewish, 111, 117
  national, 114
Mesopotamia, 80, 84
Messiah, 113 f., 179
Messianic beliefs, 183
  interpretation of, 113 f.
Middle Ages, 38, 44 f., 50, 83, 96, 103 f.
Migrations, 68, 80, 116, 128
Minorities, 65 et seq., 78, 144 f.
  admired, 67
  attitude toward majority, 67
  cultural, 65, 67
  despised, 66, 180
  elite, 67
  "inferior," 67
  Jewish, 57, 67, 79, 181
  national, 65, 67, 181
  "penalized," 68, 148, 171
  racial, 65
  religious, 65 ff., 181
  tolerance of, 65 f.
  unique, 67
"Mob spirit," 49
Moellendorf, Fritz, 62, 211
Moneylending, 82 et seq., 198
Money, significance of for Jews, 124 ff., 132, 173
  symbolic significance of, 88
Monotheism, 74, 90, 99, 163

Montaigne, 85
Moore, George Foot, 91 f., 211
Moses and Monotheism, 37, 163, 206
Mother Earth, symbolic sexual union with, 171

Napoleon, 75
Narcissism, 138 f.
Nationalism, causing anti-Semitism, 51
  Jewish, 22, 78, 146
National socialism, 55, 59, 61 f., 102 ff., 177
Nations, concept of, 75
Nazi Germany, 45, 48, 58, 158, 182 f., 200
Nazi leaders, 17, 19, 58 f., 61, 103, 183
Nazis(m), 53 et seq., 66, 71 f., 76, 86, 102, 105, 120, 145, 152 f., 177, 184
Nestorians, 68
Neurosis, 27, 29, 33, 42, 108, 131 et seq., 147, 168, 176
  and frustration, 51
  incidence of among Jews, 132 ff., 174, 178
  psychoanalytic theory of, 176
Neurotic symptoms, 26, 35, 40, 108, 131 et seq.
Neuville, H., 68, 112, 211
New Testament, 93
Normal and neurotic person, differences of, 51

Obsessional neurosis, 114, 131, 164
Occult, machinations of, 61
Oedipus complex, 27 et seq., 40, 42, 98, 109, 180, 192, 196
Ogburn, W. F., 88
Old Testament, 82, 94, 124
Omnipotence, 139
Organized masses, 48 f.
Out-group, 37, 48
Overdetermination, 65

Palestine, 22, 69 f., 80 f., 116 f., 160, 163, 166 f., 200 f.
  trauma of loss of, 162 ff., 169
Papacy, 97, 187

Paranoia, 15 et seq., 32, 61
Parkes, James W., 80, 94, 211
Parsees, 68
Passive tendencies, 33 f.
Paul, 92, 95
Pax Judaica, 59
Peguy, Charles, 21, 51, 120, 211
Persecution, in Middle Ages, 83, 167 f., 187, 195
  of Christians, 93
  of Jews, 22, 56 f., 64, 68, 70, 72, 75, 98, 120, 125, 143 f., 155, 167 ff., 173, 179, 182, 185 ff., 198
  scientific justification of, 72
Persecutor, persecuted, 63
Personality, disturbances, 108, 174, 176
  formation of, 176
  unconscious regions of, 29
Perversion, sexual, 19, 45, 72
Pharisaism, 91, 165
Pharisees, 92, 94
Philip the Fair, 83
Philistines, 70
Philo of Alexandria, 91
Phobia, 15 et seq.
Phoenicians, 80
Physical type, Jewish, 20, 25, 69, 71
Pinsker, Leon, M., 30, 211
Pirke Aboth, 92
Plot(s), Jewish, 17
  Judaeo-Masonic, 60
  mysterious, 63
Pogroms, 38, 96, 120, 136, 182
Poland, 86 f., 126, 175
Polytheism, 74
Population, Jewish, 70, 80, 115 ff., 123, 126 ff., 175
Prejudice, 18, 102, 111, 119, 143, 184
  anti-Semitic (anti-Jewish), 11, 64, 86
  causes of, 15
  in-group, 118
  latent, 20, 44, 62
  "racial," 20
Primal horde, 37
Primitive peoples, 57, 72
Projection, 32, et seq., 39, 55, 62 f., 72, 88, 99, 105, 133, 196
Propaganda, 19, 58, 62 f., 183

Protestants, protestantism, 90, 101, 122
"Protocol psychosis," 61
Protocols of the Elders of Zion, 17, 59 et seq.
Provincialism, 91
  tribal, 162
Psychoanalysis, 12, 64, 88, 104, 151, 153 et seq., 164, 175, 193
Psychoanalyst, 30, 33 f., 36, 42, 104, 107 f., 110
Psychoanalytic method, 26, 29, 37, 108, 153 f., 174
Psychoanalytic treatment, 26, 29 f., 72, 142
Psychology, collective, 12, 46
  of nations, 110, 112
Psychoses, 15, 32
Puritanism, 135

Race(s), classification of, 69
  consciousness, 157
  definition of, 68
  German, 103
  inferior, 62, 68, 183
  return to, 103, 199
Race religion, 103
Regression, 63, 177
Relativism, Jewish, 140 f.
Relativity, of national absolutes, 55
  of values, 55
Religion, "closed," 165
  Jewish, 76, 81, 84, 128 f., 135, 137, 162, 165, 166 ff.
  licit, 93, 96
  militant, 103
  philosophy of, 186
  study of, 175
Religious concepts, psychoanalysis of, 38
Religious doubts, 40, 99
Religious faith, disintegration of, 102
Religious instruction, 38 ff., 42 f., 134, 180, 192, 201
  impact of, 195 ff.
  methods of, 196 ff.
  offering solution to oedipus conflict, 192 f.
Renaissance, 102
Renan, E., 82, 90, 114, 162, 212

INDEX

Renegades, 142
Repression, 27 et seq., 34, 39, 47, 78, 99, 108, 114, 135, 150, 172, 178, 193
Resistance, 30, 36
Reversal, 55
Revolution, 11, 56, 126
  American, 75, 102
  Communist, 61
  French, 75, 102, 175
  Nazi, 105
  prehistoric, 171
Rites and ceremonies, Jewish, 114, 120, 129, 137
Rollin, Henri, 59, 118, 212
Romans, Roman Empire, 70, 74, 81 et seq., 96 f., 165
Rosenberg, Alfred, 60
Roumania, 75, 87, 115, 121
Ruppin, Arthur, 115 ff., 126 f., 212
Russell, Bertrand, 92, 212
Russia, 59 ff., 75, 87, 115, 121, 175, 182

Sachs, Hanns, 157, 212
Sacred Book, see Bible
Sadduccees, 94
Sadism, 19, 34, 55
  anal, 173
  oral, 173
Sadomasochism, 20
Sanford, R. N., 36, 204
Saracen empire, 84
Saul of Tarsus, 92
Schism, between Judaism and Christianity, 91 et seq.
Schizophrenia, 131
Second temple, 91
Semicapitalism, 82
Shammai, 167
"Sin of intention," 158
Socialism, 62, 111
Socialization, of child, 26, 38
Soil, psychological significance of, 81
  return to, 103
Solidarity, Jewish, 47, 118, 120
Spaniole, 115
Speier, Hans, 58, 209

Sphere, of consumption, 86
  of distribution, 86 f.
  of production, 86
Sphincter morality, 114
Spinoza, 85
Stonequist, E. V., 149, 212
Suggestion, 48
Suicide rate, among immigrants, 151
Superego, 29, 38 ff., 48, 99, 104 f., 155, 182, 186, 192
Super-Jews, 23
Superiority feelings, 138 ff., 156
Synagogue, 97
Syphiliphobia, 15 f.

Talmud, 82, 91 et seq., 167 f.
Temple, destruction of, 92 f., 160 ff., 166
Temporal ambitions, renunciation of, 165, 170
Tendency, to generalize, 35 f., 46
  to personify, 46
Testament of the Twelve Patriarchs, 91
Thinking, in stereotypes, 20, 24, 35
Third International, 61
Totalitarian regimes, 13, 59, 105
Toynbee, A. J., 68, 90 f., 93, 147 f., 213
Tradition(s), Christian, 103
  community of, 68
  impact of, 58, 110, 149, 155, 191 f., 197
Traits, differences in degree and distribution, 109 f., 174
  German, 114
  Jewish, 13, 21, 25, 107 et seq., 118, 148, 152, 155, 184
  Jewish, formation of, 172
  neurotic, 183
  personality, 107, 168, 198
  "racial," 174
  related to anxiety, 137
Transfer, from incestuous love object to foreigner, 73
  of guilt, 57
  of inadequacies to Jews, 57
Transference, 30 f.

Transmission, by heredity, 15, 154, 174
  by identification, 176
  by tradition, 176
  of emotions in masses, 48
Trauma, psychological, 131
Turkey, 121

Ultranationalism, 77 f.
United States, 20, 60, 67, 74 f., 89, 115 ff., 121, 123, 127, 132 ff., 143, 146, 175, 194 f., 200 f.
Universalism, 91
Usurers, Usury, 82, 97, 182, 190, 198

Violence, collective, 53
  horror of, 135
  renunciation of, 173

Waelder, Robert, 177, 213
Wandering Jew, legend of, 46, 79, 198
Wassermann, Jacob, 139, 213
William the Conqueror, 83
Wolf, Katherine, 9
World Jewry, 63, 146
World religion, 103
World War, 59, 86, 116 f., 126, 167, 200

Xenophobia, 65 f., 74, 77, 89

Yiddish, 115, 120

Zionism, 113 f., 146, 200
Zweig, Stefan, 118, 213

(Continued from front flap)

so many of the methodological pitfalls into which others have fallen in dealing with this subject—errors which have resulted in painful naïvetés. The dispassionateness is also deeply impressive. I look forward to the book with much pleasure..."

    NATHANIEL ROSS, M.D.
    New York Psychoanalytic
    Institute

———•———

ABOUT THE AUTHOR:

Dr. Loewenstein studied at the Universities of Zürich, Berlin and Paris, and has been active in the psychoanalytic movement for more than twenty-five years. He was a charter member of the Paris Psychoanalytic Society and Institute and, in collaboration with Princess Marie Bonaparte, translated Sigmund Freud's five great case histories into French. An Associate Clinical Professor of Psychiatry at Yale University, Dr. Loewenstein has for many years taught at the New York Psychoanalytic Institute of which he is now president. He has published numerous essays and articles and made many original contributions to the theory and technique of psychoanalysis.

———•———

International Universities Press, Inc.
227 West 13th Street New York 11, N. Y.

www.ingramcontent.com/pod-product-compliance
Lightning Source LLC
Chambersburg PA
CBHW031253230426
43670CB00005B/162